Curriculum Gymnastics

A teacher's guide to theory and practice

Anne Williams

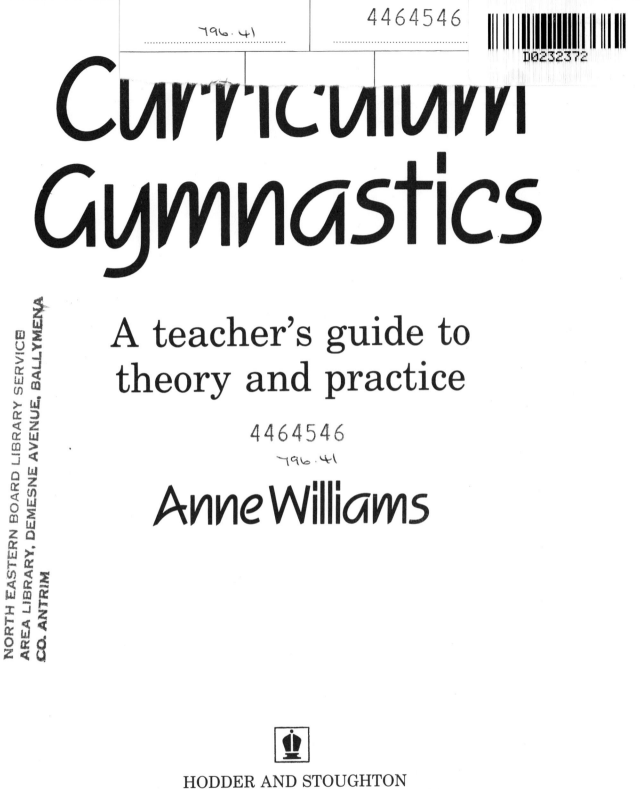

HODDER AND STOUGHTON
LONDON SYDNEY AUCKLAND TORONTO

British Library Cataloguing in Publication Data

Williams, Anne
    Curriculum gymnastics: a teacher's
    guide to theory and practice.
    1. Gymnastics—Study and teaching
    (Secondary)
    I. Title
    796.4′1   GV461

    ISBN 0-340-40427-2

First published 1987

Typeset by Tradespools Ltd, Frome
Printed and bound in Great Britain for
Hodder and Stoughton Educational,
a division of Hodder and Stoughton Ltd,
Mill Road, Dunton Green, Sevenoaks, Kent
by The Eastern Press Ltd., Reading

Contents

Acknowledgment

The author and publishers would like to thank Steve Loakes for taking the photographs used in this book and also the pupils from Harborne Hill School, Birmingham for agreeing to be photographed.

1 *Why gymnastics?*

Introduction

Gymnastics has been a part of the physical education curriculum through a period which has seen changes in the philosophy of education and in the organisation of our schools. It is identified in documents about the curriculum and about teacher preparation as one of the core areas of the physical education curriculum, along with games, dance, swimming, athletics and outdoor activities. These core activities constitute the means whereby the aims of physical education are to be achieved. In order to identify the particular contribution which gymnastics can make, the aims of physical education should perhaps be clarified. For the purposes of this book, the following aims are used as a basis for subsequent discussion. (A more comprehensive discussion of the aims of physical education may be found in *Curriculum 11– 16*, DES, 1978 and Andrews, 1978.)

1 To enable each child to maximise his physical potential through the development of basic skills of movement, balance, co-ordination and timing.

2 To promote an interest and an enjoyment of physical activity as a contribution to fitness and general well-being, and as a positive use of leisure time.

3 To develop the ability to co-operate with other people and to compete fairly and honestly.

4 To promote an interest in bodily movement as a vehicle for creative and artistic experience.

5 To promote understanding of other aspects of life through the medium of physical activity.

In order that these aims might be achieved and that a balanced programme might be offered in schools, HMI suggest 'areas of experience' which should be included in the curriculum. These form a useful means of classification by which the value and contribution of specific activities may be considered. They are:

1 areas in which the main aim is the development of skilful body management. This may be achieved through gymnastics (educational and formal or Olympic), swimming, trampolining and athletics events, as well as in activities such as judo and fencing;

2 areas in which the main aim is creating or being involved in an artistic experience through bodily movement;

3 areas in which the main aim is competition between groups and individuals involving the use of psycho-motor skills;

4 areas in which the main aim is bodily training leading to increased powers of strength, stamina, endurance and a general feeling of well-being;

5 areas in which the main aim is to meet challenging experiences in varying environments.

The aims and purposes of gymnastics are considered, therefore, in relation to the aims of physical education listed, and in relation to those areas of experience which may assist in their attainment.

Aims and purposes of gymnastics

This section considers the ways in which gymnastics may contribute to the achievement of the aims of education and of physical education. A number of possibilities are discussed, and, in some schools, given resources and commitment, it may be that all of these possibilities can be explored. In other schools, for various reasons, the curriculum time available for gymnastics may be limited, and, consequently, the number of avenues which can reasonably be explored will be restricted. In these circumstances, the aims and features which take precedence will depend upon the philosophy of the school and the physical education programme, and upon the priorities adopted by the teacher.

A number of the features claimed for gymnastics are also, of course, rightly claimed for other activities which may form a part of the physical education curriculum. It is therefore important to examine the purposes of gymnastics in a specific school, in relation to the rest of the physical education curriculum, and indeed in relation to the whole curriculum of that school. For example, it is possible to teach gymnastics in such a way that its aesthetic qualities receive great emphasis, and in a school where opportunities for aesthetic experience are severely limited, it may be entirely proper that gymnastics should be seen as a medium for the provision of this kind of experience. Another school, on the other hand, may include aesthetic experiences through art, music, dance or drama, to such an extent that other features of gymnastics may rightly be the focus of attention in that school.

Gymnastics focuses on the body. In so doing it differs from games which are concerned with manipulating other tools (rackets, sticks, balls, etc.), and which require the efficient use of the body in order to achieve the purposes of the game. Gymnastics aims specifically to develop body management and body awareness. It is concerned with bodily skill and with precision of movement and form. Work with young children concentrates upon body management in the sense of discovering possibilities and also becoming aware of capabilities and limitations. As children gain experience, demands in terms of control, finish and precision of movement can be increased. It is this concern with precision of movement and with quality of response that distinguishes gymnastics from other activities such as keep fit, circuit training and so on, which also focus on the body but which have other purposes.

The control, style and precision which characterise good quality gymnastics may readily be seen in the performance of competitive gymnastics. Curriculum gymnastics can make exactly the same demands in terms of quality of response, although the level of difficulty will obviously be significantly different. Indeed, it may be argued that unless high quality movement is demanded, then other activities might equally well fulfil many of the purposes which may be attained through the medium of gymnastics.

In addition, gymnastics can maintain or improve strength, endurance, mobility and flexibility. It is probably fair to say that this is an aspect of gymnastics which has tended to be neglected in recent years in curriculum work. There are, of course, other activities which may be included in the curriculum for the purposes of improving these particular physical qualities, in which case there may be other aspects of gymnastics which should receive more attention. Nevertheless, the development of these qualities is of interest to many children and in taking account of the needs and interests of the class, strong arguments can be made for the inclusion of these sorts of physical challenges in a gymnastics context.

So far the physical characteristics of gymnastics have been considered. Gymnastics in an educational context, is, of course, concerned with more than the acquisition of a number of specific skills and agilities, important though these are. The process of learning and consequently the teaching methods used, are of equal significance. One of the features of contemporary curriculum gymnastics is the variety of teaching methods which may be utilised. The relationship between teaching style and learning outcome is discussed in a later chapter. However, it should be noted that in order to utilise gymnastics to achieve a range of educational aims, the teacher needs to have a range of teaching styles at his disposal. The teacher who uses only a direct, didactic and teacher dominated approach may well achieve much in terms of skill acquisition and in discipline and obedience, but is less likely to produce children whose decision-making skills are well-developed, simply because his chosen method of presentation gives the child no opportunity to practise decision-making. Bearing in mind then that teaching methods affect the potential of an activity, other features and purposes of gymnastics may be considered.

As a sport form, gymnastics undoubtedly has a clear aesthetic emphasis. This is seen both in style and manner of performance of skills, and in the creation and composition of sequences. Curriculum work can also contribute to the aesthetic experience of the pupil. There are times when concentration upon this feature of gymnastics may be a powerful motivating force for a particular class or age group. At other times other aspects may be more relevant to the pupils' interests.

Much criticism levelled at contemporary physical education programmes is of the undue emphasis placed upon competition and elitism. Gymnastics' place in the curriculum may be justified on the grounds that it is one way of providing a balance between competitive and non-competitive activities. While the judicious use of competition can be a useful educational tool, and an important motivating force, intrinsically competitive activities, particularly when played to adult codes of rules, are disliked by many children, especially the less successful. Gymnastics is an area of the curriculum which offers scope for non-competitive activity, assessed according to individual improvement and progress. This is true of all gymnastics forms, in the sense that Olympic or Modern Rhythmic Gymnastics is not intrinsically competitive in the way that a game of squash or rugby is competitive. The child who is sufficiently gifted physically to cope with the high skill threshold activities of much Olympic Gymnastics work, but who dislikes competition, may nevertheless gain much satisfaction and self-esteem from mastering skills and agilities which make considerable technical demands. In curriculum work, quality of performance may be assessed without the need to produce winners and losers.

A further feature of gymnastics is that it offers scope for both individual and shared or co-operative activity. This is in contrast to team activities, which often dominate the physical education curriculum, and again enables gymnastics to contribute to providing balance in the curriculum. The individual nature of gymnastics means that it is possible to offer children the opportunity to progress at their own pace. While this feature has often been used as a major justification for including educational gymnastics in the curriculum, it should be noted that working in this way places great demands on the teacher, and that it may be that some teachers will be unable to meet these demands. It is undoubtedly very much easier to keep control and monitor progress in a situation where the whole class is working on a single activity, than in the more open situation where many different activities are going on. The opportunity for individualised work is nevertheless one of the features of gymnastics which may be exploited.

The opportunity to co-operate and share is present in many physical activities including gymnastics, where the kind of co-operation demanded is rather different from that required in, for example, the team game. Children have to share the available work space, and also the available equipment, and have to co-operate with one another in setting out or rearranging the work space. This aspect of co-operative behaviour will be present in all gymnastics work. Co-operation may also be required if partner or group work features in the gymnastics programme, and the ability to share ideas, to assist one

The individual nature of gymnastics enables children to progress at their own pace (see also pages 6 and 7)

The ability to assist one another

another and to respect the views and ideas of others may be developed through this medium.

The material of gymnastics is examined elsewhere. However, it should perhaps be said that the wealth of material available to the gymnastics teacher is such that selection can be made to suit all ages, abilities and aptitudes. This wide variety of material derives from many sources, from the work of Ling and Jahn, from that based upon Laban's principles of movement, from earlier curriculum work and from the world of sports gymnastics. In addition to this rich variety, the environment in which gymnastics is taught adds further possibilities. Resources vary greatly from school to school, but the total range of apparatus available – bars, platforms, rebound, free swinging and so on – adds to the possibilities which may be explored.

Gymnastics can therefore offer the pupil a range of experience and can contribute to various aspects of development. The contribution it can make to the physical development of the child and to the acquisition of physical skill, must be central to its purpose in the curriculum. It is physical education's and therefore gymnastics' concern with the physical which distinguishes it from other subject areas and which gives it its unique place in the curriculum. Gymnastics can, however, also play a part in other areas of development which are thought to be a part of the educational process. It may be used for the development of language, and for the application of scientific principles. Gymnastics can be a part of the child's aesthetic experience. Personal and social development can be fostered through giving opportunities for taking

Co-operation in group work

Children have to co-operate in setting out equipment

responsibility, for co-operating and sharing, and for decision-making. These features will not occur as automatic byproducts of gymnastics activity, but may occur if planned for by the teacher, assuming that some priority is given to them, and that material and method of presentation are selected accordingly.

The nature of curriculum gymnastics

Unlike other physical activities, there are significant differences between much of the work undertaken in curriculum gymnastics and that presented to the child as the adult world of competitive gymnastics work. This section considers the similarities and differences between various gymnastics forms. The term 'curriculum gymnastics' rather than 'educational gymnastics' is used because it is thought that while one would hope that any gymnastics undertaken as part of the curriculum would be educational, the title 'educational gymnastics' or 'modern educational gymnastics' has become associated with a specific approach. Its use can therefore be confusing in a discussion which, although concerned with the educational aspect of gymnastics, is not restricted to one particular style of teaching or way of organising material.

Through the 1950s and 1960s, gymnastics in the curriculum developed independently of competitive gymnastics, particularly in girls' physical education where educational gymnastics based on Laban's principles of movement had gained much ground. Boys' physical education at this time had either retained traditional vaulting and agility work or adopted the problem-solving approach advocated by Bilbrough and Jones. Following the explosion of interest which occurred in the wake of the Munich Olympic Games of 1972, various aspects of Olympic Gymnastics previously excluded from curriculum work began to appear in schools. The BAGA instituted an award scheme for schools, based on individually performed skills. Opportunities to take part in gymnastics outside school, through clubs, increased significantly, especially for girls. For some time, developments in gymnastics as a competitive medium continued apace, while curriculum gymnastics or educational gymnastics showed much less evidence of change. By the 1970s, curriculum gymnastics had been written off by some as a curriculum activity, especially in boys' work, although its popularity as a sport form had never been greater.

It is perhaps unfortunate that conflict between supporters of different gymnastics forms has led to a focus on disparities between them, where examination of common ground might not only prove more fruitful, but would also reveal that certain assumptions about the different forms are mistaken, or at least open to misinterpretation. Because gymnastics encompasses a wide range of material and because education involves many different kinds of experience, there are numerous ways in which gymnastics can be taught as an educational medium. It is therefore difficult to identify one particular approach which is 'best' for curriculum gymnastics. Furthermore, staff and resources vary and pupils enter school with widely differing abilities, interests and previous experience. Continuation of debate about gymnastics in terms of 'which way is best' seems to promise little by way of constructive suggestion about the positive contribution which gymnastics might make in a physical education programme.

There is little doubt that children are interested in gymnastics. Increased media interest has played a part, and it may be that the physical education profession has underestimated the implications for gymnastics in the curriculum, of developments outside. Changes in the world of gymnastics outside schools have maintained the impetus generated by Munich in 1972. The continued television coverage reveals ever rising standards of performance, and a broadening of the forms of competitive gymnastics into branches such as Sports Acrobatics, Modern Rhythmic Gymnastics and so on.

To choose to ignore aspects of gymnastics which may form a significant part of the pupils' experience outside school, suggests a failure to recognise the necessity to take account of the pupils' viewpoint. It is inevitable that the way pupils perceive gymnastics will be coloured by 'media' images as well as, and possibly more intensely than by the experiences offered in school. This is particularly relevant in gymnastics, which for all sorts of reasons presents a more complex problem than some other activity areas.

In many physical education activities there is an obvious relation between the curriculum activity and the 'adult' activity form. This has its disadvantages, and the problems involved in teaching, for example, soccer as an educational activity, where pupils bring a model of soccer as a competitive professional sport, could be debated at length. Nevertheless, this link does mean that the pupil can see a relevance to the activity which is not as immediately obvious where the activity appears to have little or no common ground with that practised under a similar label in the outside/adult world. In the case of gymnastics, the various award schemes promoted by the sports governing body can produce a further discrepancy between curriculum work and extra-curricular activity in schools which use the governing body award schemes in the club situation.

The implication of continuing to divorce curriculum gymnastics from that experienced by the child outside school, whether as performer or as spectator, is that curriculum gymnastics will lose ground, since forces external to the school usually combine to exert significantly greater influence on a child than those forces which can be applied by the school. Thus recognition of particular characteristics and features of contemporary competitive gymnastics as well as of curriculum gymnastics is needed.

There is much which could be common to both competitive forms of gymnastics and to curriculum work, and a number of differences are of degree rather than of kind. Furthermore, a number of features which have been claimed for educational gymnastics are, while undoubtedly educational, not peculiar to gymnastics or even to physical education. Two examples will serve to illustrate this point.

The opportunity for each child to perform and progress at his own individual pace according to his own individual standards, often put forward as a feature fundamental to educational gymnastics, is not specific to gymnastics. It should be a part of the teaching of all individual activities, and while less easy to achieve in team games, is nevertheless very much a part of the 'teaching for understanding' approach which is currently arousing much interest. It is also unfortunate that early writing on educational gymnastics tended to suggest that children would progress at their own optimum rate with minimal encouragement from the teacher, who had simply to set appropriate tasks. The demands on the teacher, if individuality is not to become synonymous with mediocrity, should not be underestimated.

Another feature claimed as an argument in favour of educational gymnastics, is the varied environment in which teaching takes place. This is contrasted with the rigidly defined and limited equipment used in competitive gymnastics. In this case, the variety of apparatus and the flexibility with which much of it is used is indeed a particular feature of this activity and is a powerful educational medium. However, the environment does not in itself make gymnastics educational. Much excellent educational gymnastics work has taken place in gymnasia equipped for Swedish gymnastics, based upon a very different philosophy. Thus while specifically designed apparatus may well

High quality whatever the level of difficulty

offer new opportunities, it is perfectly feasible to teach educational gymnastics with a minimum of equipment, or conversely, to teach very 'uneducational' gymnastics in a gymnasium lavishly equipped for all kinds of gymnastics work.

One of the objectives of curriculum gymnastics is the development of skilled body management. This is, of course, not peculiar to educational work, but is very much a feature of all branches of sports gymnastics. Unfortunately, despite its importance in educational gymnastics, much of the criticism levelled at curriculum work is of its failure to develop this aspect. The 'pick a number of basic movements and join them together to form as many sequences as possible' approach is criticised by Groves (1973) who also points out that this approach all too often leads to a situation where children lose enthusiasm because they lack challenge. Conversely, competitive or sports gymnastics is often claimed to lack relevance in the class situation because of its high skill threshold.

All too often there appears to be a failure to make a sufficiently clear distinction between 'quality' and 'difficulty'. No one would challenge the fact that many of the skills of Olympic Gymnastics are extremely demanding technically, or that they have a very high skill threshold. Observation of many school lessons, however, suggests that there is often a failure to appreciate that high quality can be achieved where the level of difficulty is low, just as much as in actions which make great technical demands. The achievement of skilled body management implies high quality performance and should be of just as much concern to the school gymnastics teacher as to the competitive gymnastics coach. The levels of difficulty demanded may well differ. The competitive gymnast needs to acquire skills of preordained levels of difficulty in order to meet the requirements laid down by the sport's governing body. The school gymnastics teacher is not bound by these constraints. In any case, the size of the normal class means that concentration on actions requiring a 1:1 teaching situation is simply not an effective use of the teacher's time and expertise. The freedom which the teacher has to select from our rich gymnastics heritage is potentially one of the great strengths of curriculum gymnastics. However, the emphasis should be upon careful selection so that high quality work is produced whatever the difficulty level.

There is no doubt that in the early stages of educational gymnastics, skill teaching was sacrificed in the interests of allowing individuals to develop at their own pace, and, in the process of moving away from the rigidity of traditional work with its high failure rate, some of the good features of such work disappeared along with the bad. Indeed, one of the chief problems of educational gymnastics has arisen from the mistaken belief that individual differences can only be catered for if very wide ranging tasks are set. In fact, many tasks may be very tightly constrained and still allow achievement and balance throughout the ability range. In attempting to strike a balance between improving quality and extending range of movement, sports gymnastics can set an example which could profitably be followed in curriculum work. All competitive gymnastics requires both demonstration of particular levels of skill and of the ability to produce well structured and harmonious sequences. These two play a significant part in competitive gymnastics and a comparable balance is equally relevant in curriculum work. The production of endless sequences without the opportunity to acquire some specific skills may be compared with expecting the child to write pages of sentences without teaching him any vocabulary. Because the teacher in the school is not constrained by external demands in terms of very specific skills, the choice of material to be taught can be very much wider and can be adapted to suit the abilities of the children.

Many of the publications on educational gymnastics concentrate chiefly on the material to be used, much of which derives from Laban's movement principles, developed into a thematic approach. It has been suggested that this emphasis on content has tended to divert attention from the real key to educational gymnastics, namely the process of learning, or the style of teaching as noted by HMI:

> Gymnastics in education is not concerned only with the acquisition of a number of specific and identifiable skills or agilities although many or some will be achieved. The process by which these and other skills are learnt is of equal if not greater significance. It is important that a variety of methods or situations is used to allow all pupils to experience satisfaction and success and to develop understanding and appreciation of what the body is doing and when.

It is suggested that it is this which is the major difference between curriculum work and sports forms of gymnastics, which by their nature and because of the constraints imposed by governing body rulings, focus more on the end product than on the process by which it is achieved. This is evident in the different criteria used for their assessment. In competitive gymnastics, the performer with the highest mark is deemed to be the best. Curriculum work can be assessed not only in terms of level of skill attained, but also according to factors such as progress made, effort, understanding acquired and ability to apply knowledge gained.

As far as the material of gymnastics is concerned, the distinction between curriculum work and sports gymnastics need not be a difference in kind. The real difference lies in the freedom from governing body constraints enjoyed by the class teacher. Evaluation of a child's achievement can be in relation to his ability rather than according to preordained conventions in terms of technical requirements or style. Additionally, this freedom means that the teacher can build on the child's strengths and avoid focusing to excess on his weaknesses. What is important, however, is that this freedom is used to exploit abilities and not as an excuse for mediocrity. It is equally important that technical requirements needed for progression to more advanced work are understood, so that freedom of choice does not militate against future progress.

The lack of competition in educational gymnastics work is often cited as a point in its favour. It is perhaps unfortunate that this aspect of the work, which can indeed provide a welcome change from the competitive and elitist features of much of the physical education programme, is sometimes set in contrast to Olympic and other sports forms of gymnastics. What should perhaps be remembered is that an activity such as Olympic gymnastics is not intrinsically competitive in the same way as a game such as rugby or badminton. Indeed, many schools run very successful Olympic gymnastics clubs without ever exposing members to competition. The motivating force which is provided for some by the stimulus of competition can be provided for others by display work.

Two features of sports forms of gymnastics have tended not to feature in curriculum work. They could, and perhaps should feature more prominently.

All branches of sports gymnastics require the development of physical qualities such as flexibility, strength, mobility and endurance. Although they have been absent from most educational gymnastics programmes, their development seems to be entirely consistent with the purposes of educational gymnastics including, as Morison suggests, 'to develop each individual's latent movement powers as far as possible'. The inclusion of work in this area, as part of gymnastics, seems to be entirely in keeping with current philosophies of physical education, particularly in view of the emphasis placed on promoting active lifestyles and health related fitness. Groves is not alone in mourning the demise of vigorous exercise in educational gymnastics lessons, and the maintenance or improvement of flexibility, strength and endurance seems quite consistent with the stated aims of gymnastics, even if it is difficult to find evidence of its use in practice.

All forms of competitive gymnastics also include an aesthetic element which is a central part of this activity. Curriculum gymnastics can share this focus on the aesthetic at a level appropriate to the group or individual concerned. For some participants, the aesthetic aspect of gymnastics may be the primary motivating force and should be exploited as such. At other times, while aesthetic qualities may be recognised and encouraged, they may not be appropriate as a first priority, either for motivation or in assessing achievement.

Whether gymnastics is the most suitable vehicle for the development of the above two features is a separate issue. It could well be argued that for the older child these objectives of physical education could and should be achieved through the medium of activities which are more likely to be continued beyond the years of schooling. Nevertheless, if gymnastics is to be included in the curriculum, its potential in these areas should be exploited alongside other aims and objectives.

Ultimately, gymnastics in the curriculum is a means whereby some of the aims of physical education may be achieved. These aims in turn reflect those of the total educational process. The fact that gymnastics in one form or another has until comparatively recently enjoyed a central place in the physical education curriculum suggests that it has not only been seen as educational, but also that it has been capable of adapting to the changing demands of society. At the present time, much thought is being given to making the whole curriculum more relevant to the needs of the young people who are now leaving school and entering a society which has changed significantly over recent years, and which continues to change. In this context, physical education's contribution to the personal and social development of the child as well as to his physical development is receiving much attention. Gymnastics as a curriculum activity has considerable potential provided that the implications of developments elsewhere for the curriculum are recognised and utilised to the benefit of curriculum work. It is equally important to be clear about the nature of the features which make gymnastics 'educational' and to recognise that there are many ways in which the material of gymnastics can be presented which exploit the potential of this activity as an educational tool. Finally, it should be recognised that the teaching styles implicit in a philosophy which puts the child's needs as a priority are more difficult to sustain than are traditional teaching methods, and demand very much more from the teacher. It may be said, however, that the rewards are correspondingly greater.

2 | *The material of gymnastics*

Before detailed consideration of curriculum content can begin, an understanding of the material of gymnastics is needed, so that any selection of content may be made with an awareness of how what is chosen relates to the whole field of gymnastic activity. Just as discussion of the nature of curriculum gymnastics is hampered by focusing on disparities rather than by seeking similarities and common ground, so understanding of the material of gymnastics may be hindered if classifications of isolated approaches to its teaching are developed to the exclusion of aspects which do not fit into a particular approach. This may be seen if some classifications of educational gymnastics are examined. In concentrating on this particular approach to teaching, the 'traditional' skills of gymnastics are all too easily excluded completely, rendering such an approach quite unnacceptable to those who value skill acquisition.

Curriculum gymnastics in England has used classifications of material based upon anatomical considerations, upon the effects of activities upon the body and upon Laban's movement principles.

Anatomical considerations formed the basis of many early classifications of gymnastics material. Curriculum work in England during the early part of this century was based upon the Swedish system developed by P.H. Ling, whose influence may be seen in English PT syllabuses. The 1909 Syllabus, for example, divides exercises into:

1 introductory exercises;
2 trunk bending backward and forward;
3 arm bending and stretching;
4 balance exercises;
5 shoulder blade exercises;
6 abdominal exercises;
7 trunk turning and bending sideways;
8 marching, running, jumping, games, etc.;
9 breathing exercises.

The system of exercising each part of the body in turn was retained in the 1933 Syllabus. While *Moving and Growing* and *Planning the Programme* (Ministry of Education, 1952 and 1953), marked a significant departure from such rigidly laid down guidelines, a framework was still offered (to those teachers who desired one) in which anatomical considerations were retained:

1 general activity;
2 compensatory movements;
   (a) trunk movements;
   (b) arm and shoulder girdle movements;
   (c) foot and leg movements;
3 agility movements.

Dissatisfaction in some quarters with the limitations of purely anatomical considerations led to classifications of activities based upon the effects of activities on the body. In the 1930s both Knudsen and Bukh divided activities according to their effect on the development of strength, suppleness and agility. Endurance or stamina has also featured in this kind of classification. It is probably true to say that these aspects of gymnastics were of more interest to male physical educationists than to females. Nevertheless, *Planning the Programme* acknowledges the relevance of this kind of classification for many teachers when noting that a framework based upon terms such as mobility, strength and agility has often been found useful.

Both of these classifications see gymnastics as a system of exercises. Development of gymnastics as a sport was quite separate, stemming from Jahn's work in Germany and virtually disappearing from Britain as Ling's system was adopted by the Ministry of Education. Munrow's comments made in 1955, serve to underline the extent of the separation.

> In England the word gymnastics has become inseparably connected with the system and the sport has declined almost to the point where a name is no longer necessary for it. Brave enthusiasts who urge its revival – may success crown their efforts – now give it the name Olympic Gymnastics.

It is perhaps small wonder that skills associated with sports gymnastics received so little attention when Laban's work began to have a major influence on curriculum work in the 1950s and 1960s. Laban's classification of movement was intended to be all-embracing, although his own writing was with reference to dance and to industry. Many educational gymnastics texts use Laban's work either explicitly or implicitly. One of the earliest to put pen to paper was Ruth Morison who went on to publish a more comprehensive text in 1969. After pointing out that the material of educational gymnastics was drawn from the natural everyday activities of children, she discusses three factors to which she gives equal importance:

1 bodily aspects of action;
2 dynamic aspects of action;
3 spatial aspects of action.

To these may be added relationships, that is, partner and group work. The material therefore corresponds to Laban's classification of dance work into Body, Effort, Space and Relationship. From this very general classification, material is organised thematically. Unfortunately, themes suggested by writers not only vary, but also, at times, contain some inconsistencies. It is difficult for the inexperienced to understand how the same action can appear as 'locomotion' in one classification, as 'weight transference' in another and as 'turning' in a third. More seriously perhaps are divisions such as 'twisting and turning' where actions which involve twisting when examined biomechanically (for example, full turn jump) are taught as part of work on turning.

Nevertheless, the thematic approach, underpinned by Laban's movement principles dominated women's gymnastics teaching during this period (see, for example, Maulden and Layson, 1979 and Williams, 1973). It is interesting to note, however, that the LCC's publication on educational gymnastics, while using a thematic structure and Laban's motion factors, continues to advocate the division of tasks within a lesson into 'whole body', 'work with weight supported on the arms', and 'leg work', thereby retaining some element of more formal work. More typical of the content analysis of educational gymnastics would be Morison's:

Actions emphasising locomotion:
1   transfer of weight (rocking, rolling, steplike actions, sliding);
2   travelling (on different body parts, at different speeds, moving and stopping, in different directions and using different pathways);
3   flight (take off, flight, landing, single and double take offs, from other body parts, shapes, landing on one or two legs, on hands, while turning, assisted).

Actions emphasising balance:
1   weightbearing;
2   balancing skills;
3   arriving (moving to hold a balance);
4   on and off balance.

Control of movement emphasising:
1   bodily aspects through bend/stretch/twist/turn/shapes/symmetry/asymmetry;
2   dynamic aspects;
3   spatial aspects.

Relationships in partner and group work.

Male physical educationists were in the main sceptical of the approach adopted by female members of the profession. The apparent disregard of mobility, strength and endurance was questioned, as was the omission of teaching specific agilities. It is, however, difficult to find men's work based upon any systematic classification. Much was based on vaulting and agility, utilising aspects of sports gymnastics (with some adaptations) traceable to quite different roots from that underpinning other work. Where a problem-solving approach was adopted (as in the work of Bilbrough and Jones, 1973 and John Cope, 1967), lessons tended to retain the sort of structure advocated by the LCC, retaining a balance through ensuring that tasks exercised the whole body fairly systematically.

Recent thinking about the material of gymnastics has been influenced by a number of factors. The growth in participation in sports gymnastics and in TV coverage of it has led to far greater awareness of, and knowledge about, the content of competitive work. Physical education teachers are no longer trained in single sex institutions and consequently the differences in approach between the sexes which were so evident in the 1950s and 1960s have lessened. The time available for gymnastics in higher education institutions has, in most cases, decreased.

A classification of gymnastics material

The classification which follows provides a logical ordering of material which is not restricted to a specific approach or method. It draws heavily upon the work of John Wright (1980). Those anatomical and kinesiological factors which assist in providing a logical ordering of actions are utilised. It also incorporates Laban's classification of movement in order to give due attention to those aspects of space, dynamics and relationships which augment, arise from or modify actions of the whole body or of body parts. By drawing on these different features, it is possible to offer a classification of material which may be used to describe, analyse or structure gymnastics in any context, and into which any gymnastics movement may be placed. In considering curriculum gymnastics, it will be necessary to select from the material which could be utilised, and selection of material is discussed later. Table 2.1 summarises the material which is described in greater detail in the following pages.

A Actions

Gymnastics is first and foremost action, in that without the action of the body or of body parts there can be no spatial, dynamic or relationship variable. Understanding of the actions of both the whole body and of body parts, and of the relationship between the two is thus fundamental.

1 Whole body positions
Held positions are used in many gymnastics situations. They may be a starting point or a finishing position. They are frequently adopted, particularly in competition or display work, as demonstrations of strength, mobility, balance or a combination of all three.

Table 2.1 Gymnastics material classified

(a) Action	(b) Space	(c) Dynamics	(d) Relationships

1 *Whole body positions*
   (i)   in different relationships to point(s) of support
   (ii) Using different body parts as support
   (iii) stable or unstable
	1 Personal space
	2 General space
	3 Direction
	4 Level
	5 Height and distance
	6 Pathway
		1 Speed
		2 Timing
		3 Use of appropriate effort or force
			1 To floor
			2 To apparatus
			3 To other people

2 *Whole body actions – travelling* rolling stepping/step-like springing assisted springing swinging flying dropping sliding part-circling combinations of the above			
3 *Whole body actions – non-travelling* circling pivoting step turning spinning swing turning free flight turning lifting lowering tilting/leaning waving swinging rocking springing in place combinations of the above			
4 *Combinations of 1, 2 & 3*			
5 *Actions of body parts* bend/stretch open/close circle/partcircle/swing twist shoulder elevation/depression combinations of the above			
6 *Functions of body part actions* initiate/maintain/accelerate decelerate/redirect/arrest motion change direction/pathway/plane change relationship of whole body to floor/apparatus/other gymnasts change relationship of gymnast's body parts			

Held positions are frequently used

They may be considered

(a) in relation to the point or points of support.
    (i) beneath points of support (for example, hangs from high bar, front and rear scale on rings);
    (ii) above points of support (for example, handstand on box, bars, front rest on bar, floor balances);
    (iii) to side of points of support;
    (iv) various combinations from (i), (ii) and (iii).

(b) in terms of their relative stability.
Positions fall broadly into two categories, namely,
    relatively *stable*;
    relatively *unstable*.
Relatively unstable positions are commonly called *balances*. The stability of any held position depends on several factors:
    (i) the position of the centre of gravity – this must be over the supporting base if the position is to be maintained,
    (ii) the lower the centre of gravity is, the more stable the position,
    (iii) the larger the supporting base, the more stable the position.

Thus a large base such as the back is stable, and so is a base using four small points of support, such as hands and feet, spread over a wide area. In contrast, a balance on one hand is unstable and difficult to maintain. A headstand on the floor is easier than a headstand on a beam because the three points of support can be spread more widely on the floor than on a beam.

(c) in terms of body parts used:
    foot/feet;   legs;   trunk;
    hands;   arms;   head/neck.

2 Whole body actions – travelling

(a) rolling – any action where the body weight is taken in succession by adjacent body parts or by parts which have been made adjacent such as in placing the feet adjacent to the hips in order to complete a forward roll to stand;

(b) stepping and step-like (for example, climbing) – actions where a body part is removed and replaced (either the same body part as in walking on the hands, or a different body part as in a walkover). All walking actions are included (on feet and on hands); stepping may be from other parts, for example, from knee to knee or include wheeling actions such as cartwheel;

(c) springing – all actions where the body is launched into the air so that travel occurs in free flight. Thus jumps are included in this category, with various take-offs and landings, also springing from feet to hands as in dive rolls, or from hands (or head and hands) to feet as in many traditional vaults, such as headspring, handspring and so on. Somersaults and other aerial movements also come into this category;

(d) assisted springing – where the spring is assisted, the body does not break contact with the floor or apparatus. There is, however, a sudden increase in force which differentiates this category from stepping or step-like actions. A handstand from a double foot take off onto a box or bench would come into this category;

(e) swinging – this uses a pendulum action in order to travel, for example, using a rope to cross from a bench to a beam;

(f) flying (from swing or being thrown) – flying as a result of being thrown is seen to great effect in Sports Acrobatics work where one partner throws the other into somersaults to the floor or to be recaught. This kind of free flight may also be achieved from a rope or bar by letting go before landing;

(g) dropping – a method of travelling down, for example, simply releasing a high bar and dropping to the floor;

(h) sliding – sloping apparatus is the most obvious choice for this activity, although it can also take place on a suitable floor surface. The part in contact with the floor or apparatus remains in contact and reduction in friction is required for travel to take place;

(i) part-circling (with one or more than one directional orientation) – for example, a roll from a top bar to a bottom bar travels but is not a complete circle;

(j) combinations of the above – these may be simple or complex.

All of the above categories may be performed with or without turning around specified axes, for example, jumps may be performed with or without turn, sliding down a bench may be performed with or without turning and so on.

3 Whole body actions – non-travelling

Unlike the actions described in 2, the following are performed without travel, on one spot.

(a) circling – the body does not travel but moves around a fixed axis, for example, a back hip circle round a bar;

(b) pivoting from balance position – often used to lead into travel, for example, fall to prone, or one leg start, pivot forward (followed by forward roll);

(c) step turning in place – pirouetting on the hands is an excellent example of this where the body part is removed and replaced but without travel; similarly step turns may be performed using the feet;

(d) spinning – like sliding, the same point of contact is retained and the body rotates using reduction in friction;

(e) swing turning – for example, on a rope or from a single hand reverse hang on a bar;

(f) free flight turning – twisting somersaults, turning jumps performed on the spot;

(g) lifting – for example, from a headstand lift to handstand;

(h) lowering – many situations where the body is lowered, for example, from a head or handstand;

(i) tilting/leaning/swaying – a feature of much of Modern Rhythmic work;

(j) waving – sometimes seen in women's competitive floor work, also seen often in dance where a body wave is used to, for example, rise to the feet;

(k) swinging – a pendulum swing for example on a bar, with no travel, often a preparation for something else;

(l) rocking – also often a preparation for rolling and to build momentum;

(m) springing in place – all jumps on the spot, somersaults on the spot, spotted flic flacs and so on;

(n) simple and more complex combinations of the above.

4 Combinations of 1, 2 and 3

5 Actions of body parts

Particular body parts or segments play a crucial role in making certain things possible and in making modifications to actions, for example, the actions of various body parts open up the possibilities of many different endings to a forward roll. If in rolling round a bar both hands are placed on the same side of the body instead of the more usual one on each side, the action will be significantly modified. They may be classified into types of action as follows. The functions of the body parts are discussed in 6.

(a)   bend, stretch/straighten type;
(b)   open, close type;
(c)   circle, part circle, swing type;
(d)   twist type;
(e)   elevation/depression (shoulders);
(f)   blends of the above.

Additionally, static muscle contractions are especially significant to the maintenance of various whole body and part body positions.

6   Functions of body parts

These occur in the context of whole body positions and/or actions. The actions of body parts listed in 5 serve various purposes. They may:

(a)   initiate, maintain, accelerate, decelerate, redirect, arrest motion (thereby determining the flow and rhythm of motion);
(b)   change direction, pathway, plane and level of motion of whole body and of particular body parts;
(c)   change relationship of whole body to floor, apparatus, other gymnasts (includes effect on extension of body and on the planes in which motion and stillness occur);
(d)   change relationships of gymnast's body parts (i.e. determine body form, shape).

They are best considered as:

(i)   body parts in contact (or about to make contact with floor, apparatus, other gymnasts, which maintain, increase or decrease applications of force through actions from 5a to 5f to cause: gripping, releasing, supporting, sliding, pulling, pushing, otherwise imparting impetus (for example, to rope). For instance, if, from a headstand, an even push is applied by both hands, the result will be a symmetrical forward roll. If, however, one hand pushes harder than the other the result will be quite different;

(ii)   body parts free from contact (or about to break contact with floor, apparatus, other gymnasts). They will often work by moving the centre of gravity through the action of a body part away from the supporting base. For example, from an arabesque or Y scale, the movement of an arm or the free leg can alter the position of the centre of gravity and

thereby initiate a roll forwards. Body parts may:
- make contact to receive and/or support;
- change body form thereby affecting the position of the body's mass centre and the position of the vertically acting line of gravity (sometimes thereby causing gravity to set up or assist motion of the whole body);
- initiate force in particular body parts and then, by sudden checking, cause their momentum to be transferred to the whole body;
- lead the whole body in particular directions through the actions given in 5a to 5f.

B Spatial aspects

Spatial aspects are concerned with where action takes place. Appreciation of spatial aspects of movement, while not fundamental in the way that action itself is, can nevertheless enhance gymnastics performance and understanding in various ways:

(a)   safety – at a very basic level, the ability to share and maximise the use of the available working space is necessary for safe performance;

(b)   variety – consideration of spatial factors can help to widen the gymnast's vocabulary by drawing attention to new possibilities, for example, performing the same skill in a variety of directions, or at different levels;

(c)   precision – movements can be performed with much greater accuracy and, in some cases, more successfully if the gymnast is able to judge where in space actions or parts of actions are to take place. For example, the placing of the feet near to or far away from the hips has a fundamental effect on the difficulty of standing up at the end of a forward roll. The ability to judge height and distance is necessary for success in much apparatus work;

(d)   balance in composition – spatial aspects may complement action considerations in the composition of sequences. For example, a floor exercise will be enriched by a balanced use of different levels, directions and pathways.

These may be achieved through focus on various aspects of spatial orientation.

1   Orientation in personal space, that is, the space immediately surrounding the body – effective use of personal space is related mainly to precision, in that an awareness of exactly where to direct the movement of the whole body or of specific parts will lead to much greater accuracy and to more harmonious and aesthetically satisfying movement. The placing of the hands well ahead of the feet in preparation for a handstand or handspring

is an example of precise placing in space improving the efficiency of the skill being performed.

2   Orientation in general space – general space refers to the available working environment, usually gymnasium or hall for gymnastics. Effective use of this space is necessary for safety, especially in the class situation where a restricted area may well have to be shared by a relatively large number of pupils. Children have to be taught to use the available space sensibly and efficiently, first for safety, and then in such a way that all are able to achieve the maximum amount of work possible.

3   Use of different directions – direction may be changed either by turning to face a new way and then moving off in that direction, or by facing the same way while moving forwards, backwards or sideways. The versatility which the ability to change direction brings can enhance safe use of space and will also enrich the movement vocabulary by adding variety.

4   Use of different levels – high, medium and low levels are all used in gymnastics, although high and low are probably more important than medium. The essence of gymnastics is more likely to be captured in actions which use agility to move from high to low, and vice versa. Change of level is an important element in creating interesting and dynamic movement.

5   Appreciation of height and distance – these aspects of space are mainly related to judgements which have to be made in placing and use of apparatus.

6   Use of varied pathways – in space may be related to:
    (a) floor pattern;
    (b) air pattern.
    Floor pattern refers to the track or pathway made on the floor. It is seen clearly in the patterns followed in Olympic Gymnastics floorwork. Attention to floor pattern in group work can help to create sequences which enable all members of the group to perform without hindering or blocking the efforts of others.
        Pathway of the body in space can be observed by following a body part. Analysis of this kind of pathway is often carried out by recording the position of the centre of gravity throughout a movement. Awareness of the pattern through space may help in skill learning, for example, understanding that a flic flac should follow a long low pathway not a short high one.

C   Dynamic aspects

Dynamics are concerned with how actions are performed. Factors such as speed, and timing of effort are critical to success in many gymnastics skills. The combination of speed and timing of effort are shown very clearly in competitive gymnastics vaulting. Timing can also be seen in work on the high and asymmetric bars. Both are relevant at a much more basic level.

(a)   Speed – actions may be performed at varying speeds. Performing quickly facilitates some actions and hinders others. For example, the beginner will find a cartwheel easier to perform fairly quickly than very slowly. On the other hand, a headstand is most easily achieved by moving into it very slowly in the early stages.

(b)   Timing – timing can be a substitute for strength in some actions; in others it is critical to success. For example, headstand lift to handstand can be achieved simply through strength: with timing of effort the same action can be performed with use of relatively little strength.

(c)   Use of appropriate force or effort – the beginner frequently feels the need to put in maximum effort in order to complete a movement. As the gymnast gains in experience, the appropriate amount of effort can be utilised, in the appropriate direction. For example, beginners learning a backward roll will often misdirect their effort by shooting their legs upwards instead of keeping a tucked shape which directs the effort over to the floor. Early attempts at a flic flac are frequently misdirected.

Detailed understanding of the dynamic aspects of movement requires a knowledge of biomechanics which is outside the scope of this book. *Gymnastics – a Mechanical Understanding* by Tony Smith goes into various elements of biomechanics in some detail.

D   Relationships

Relationship may be analysed in terms of floor, apparatus or other people. It may also be considered in relation to action, spatial and dynamic aspects of gymnastics. Its consideration may enrich and add variety to individual work. Partner and group work, where relationship to other people is central, opens up a whole new range of possibilities. It is seen in competitive gymnastics in Sports Acrobatics. In curriculum work the assistance of partner or groups may enable the gymnast to experience movements beyond their ability when attempted alone.

(a)   relationship to floor includes:
    (i)   right way up or inverted;
    (ii)   front, back or side facing.

(b)   relationship to apparatus includes:
    (i)   front back or side facing;
    (ii)   above, below or to side of apparatus;
    (iii) right way up or inverted.

(c)   relationship to partner or group includes:
        (i)   passive (support, obstacle) or active;
        (ii)   facing, back to back, side by side and so on;
        (iii)   moving in unison or in canon;
        (iv)   performing similar or dissimilar actions.

3 Gymnastics tasks

This chapter examines in more detail some of the aspects of gymnastics material discussed in the previous chapter, and provides a selection of tasks which might be set for children. The material chosen includes gymnastics actions, from the classification given, which are considered to be suitable for mixed ability groups, and also certain actions such as rolling and taking the weight on the hands, which are considered to be fundamental to the development of skill. In the main, spatial, dynamic and relationship aspects are included as added dimensions to the various actions. Partner work, however, is taken as a section in its own right, since this particular area is seen as having great potential as a separate area of work as well as being one way of developing other aspects of the work. Under each heading, a brief analysis of material which might be included is followed by tasks for floor work and for apparatus work. The level of specificity varies from task to task. However, no specific teaching style is implied. For example, the first task suggested under the heading of 'Balance' is 'Balance on many different body parts'. This could be presented to the class in several different ways as follows:

1 The teacher could demonstrate a number of different balances which the class then copies.

2 The teacher could ask the class to find as many different balances as possible.

3 The teacher could make a series of work cards available, each showing a selection of balances at varying levels of difficulty. The pupils would then work through each card in turn, using the pictures as models.

4 The teacher could present the class with a list of possible points of support and ask the class to find balances on each of them.

There are other possibilities. Different teaching styles are discussed at greater length in Chapter 5.

The language used is not intended for presentation to the child. Appropriate language and terminology will vary according to the age and ability of the class, and according to the preferences of the teacher. Effective teaching is most likely to take place where the teacher has a rich and varied terminology on which to call.

A number of the tasks given make reference to specific basic gymnastic skills. The teaching points and progressions for some of these are given in the following chapter for those teachers who wish to spend some time developing these core skills. Other specific skills which could be taught as part of each area are also given. These include some very basic skills suitable for introduction as a class activity, and also some more difficult skills more suitable for introduction to groups within a class, depending on ability.

1 Travelling (Locomotion)

Travelling involves moving from one place to another using various body parts and different body actions.

Travel using different body parts may include:

feet (walk, run, skip, hop, etc.);
hands and feet;
other small body parts (knee, elbow, etc.);
hands only (more likely on apparatus than on floor);
large body surfaces.

Travel using different body actions can include:

running;
jumping;
sliding;
rolling;
stepping;
swinging;
turning;
twisting;

Tasks:

1 Run about using all the space.
2 Run and stop on command.
3 Run on spot; when teacher says 'change' run anywhere; when teacher says 'change' run on spot and so on.
4 Run very slowly; when teacher says 'change' run very quickly and so on.
5 Run using very small steps; when teacher says 'change' use large steps and so on.
6 Run sideways.
7 Run backwards.

8 Run, changing direction on command.
9 Move about space using hands and feet.
10 Move about space using other body parts.
11 Move about space changing body parts used when teacher says 'change'.
12 Move about space changing body parts as named by teacher.
13 Roll across mat in different ways.
14 Roll into a different finishing position.
15 Roll, step, roll and finish.
16 Roll, spin and step out of the spin.
17 Spin, step and roll.
18 Practise a specific action using hands and feet.
19 Travel using hands and feet then roll.
20 Travel linking hands and feet, a spin, and a roll in any order.
21 Run, jump and land.
22 Jump as far as possible.
23 Run, jump, spin and roll.
24 Run, jump, turn and slide (if surface is suitable).
25 Link a jump, a roll and an action using hands and feet.
26 Choose three different kinds of travel and make up a sequence using each action twice.

Using benches and mats:

1 Run along bench forwards.
2 Hop along bench.
3 Run along bench backwards.
4 Move along bench using hands and feet.
5 Slide along bench.
6 Slide to middle of bench, spin and roll off onto mat.
7 Run along bench and jump off the end.
8 Run to halfway and jump off sideways.
9 Run and jump over bench.
10 Roll off bench or over bench.
11 Run, jump off bench, land and roll.
12 Cross bench using hands and feet.
13 Cross bench so that both hands are on bench.
14 Cross bench so that one hand is on bench and one hand is on floor.
15 Link different movements to travel along bench, across part of floor and across mat.
16 Link a jump, a roll, an action using hands and feet and a slide to make a sequence which uses bench, mat and floor.

Cross bench so that both hands are on bench

On apparatus:

Different pieces of large apparatus open up new possibilities, for example, travelling using hands only on ropes or bars, swinging, climbing, gripping and releasing on ropes, hanging, gripping and swinging on bars and wall bars.

1 Travel along and off apparatus.
2 Travel over apparatus.
3 Travel to apparatus onto it and off it.
4 Roll along boxes and around bars.
5 Balance along narrow surfaces.
6 Climb up or along ropes/window ladders.
7 Travel along high bars hanging under bar.
8 Travel over the top of double beams, through the space and under the lower bar.
9 Travel along or over apparatus using hands and feet only.
10 Travel up to, over and away from aparatus using rolling, jumping and taking weight on hands and feet, to make a sequence.
11 Travel round your own apparatus circuit using a different form of travelling on each piece.
12 Travel round circuit so that you never touch the floor.
13 Travel round the circuit so that you use apparatus and floor alternately.
14 Travel onto your apparatus and jump off.
15 Travel onto apparatus and get off so that you take your weight onto your hands.
16 Make up a sequence using all pieces of apparatus arrangement to include travel using hands only, travel by rolling and a jump off apparatus.

2 Rolling activities

Rolling includes:
(a) skills of forward roll; backward roll; sideways roll; fish/chest roll; circle roll; other activities (see work cards).

(b) rolling from different starting positions, for example, forward roll – from two feet standing, one foot standing, crouch, straddle, arabesque, handstand, backward roll from crouch – two feet standing, one foot standing, long sitting, straddle.

(c) rolling to different finishing positions, for example, forwards to two feet, one foot, straddle, lie flat, 'V' sit, splits, into handstand.

(d)   rolling from one starting position to the same finishing position, for example, crouch to crouch, straddle to straddle.

(e)   rolling from one starting position to a different finishing position, for example, crouch to one foot stand, straddle to splits.

(f)   rolling at different speeds.

(g)   rolling onto, off, along, over, round apparatus.

Tasks:

1   Roll to finish standing on two feet.
2   Roll in a different direction to finish standing on two feet.
3   Roll to finish standing on one foot.
4   Roll to a different finishing position.
5   Roll forwards and add a twist at the end to finish on two knees or one knee.
6   Roll forwards to finish in a long sit or straddle sit.
7   Roll forwards to finish lying flat.
8   Roll forwards to finish in a 'V' sit.
9   Roll backwards onto one knee.
10   Roll backwards onto two feet.
11   Roll sideways (a) tucked and (b) stretched.
12   Roll sideways so that only your shoulders make contact with the floor.
13   Find a different starting position, roll and finish standing on two feet.
14   Find a different starting position and roll to finish in the position you started from.
15   Roll so that you start in one position and finish in a contrasting position.
16   Jump, land and roll forwards.
17   Half turn jump, land and roll backwards.
18   Roll, followed by stretch jump.
19   Roll followed by turning jump.
20   Full turn jump, land and roll forwards.
21   Roll, spin and step out of roll.
22   Step, roll and spin.
23   Step, roll and jump.
24   Perform the same roll, first very slowly and then very quickly.
25   Perform three different rolls, alternating slow, quick, slow.

Using benches and mats:

1   Start on bench and roll onto mat.
2   Start on mat or floor and roll to finish on bench.

3 Roll along bench.
4 Jump off bench, land and roll on mat.
5 Dive forward roll over bench.
6 Roll to arrive at bench, balance on bench and roll off in a different direction.
7 Travel half way along bench and roll onto mat.
8 Roll so that you travel parallel to bench, quarter turn and cross bench.
9 Roll towards bench, quarter turn and travel along bench.
10 Balance on floor or mat, roll to finish in a different balance on bench.

On apparatus:

1 Get onto apparatus, jump off and roll on mat.
2 Get over apparatus, land and roll on mat.
3 Roll along apparatus.
4 Roll onto apparatus.
5 Roll off apparatus.
6 Roll round apparatus (where applicable).
7 Jump onto apparatus, roll along or off.
8 Step to get onto apparatus, roll round it, get off and roll on mat.
9 Roll to arrive at apparatus, get on using hands and feet, roll on or round apparatus and get off.
10 Balance on apparatus, put hands onto the floor and roll off.
11 Use apparatus to show rolls in three different directions linked to make a sequence.
12 Find two rolls that you can perform slowly on apparatus and two you can perform quickly.

Apparatus opens up many new possibilities, for example, bars for rolling round. It is important to consider whether the apparatus is suitable for the task being set. In many schools the available apparatus is such that different arrangements require the setting of different tasks.

Specific skills which could be included:

backward roll to straddle;
forward roll to straddle;
circle roll;
back roll through handstand;
dive forward roll.

There are many others.

3 Balancing Activities

Balance implies holding a position of stillness. Weightbearing is an elementary aspect of balance involving supporting the body's weight, but implying the need for rather less skill than that needed to hold a balance. A balance normally refers to the holding of an unstable position. This section includes both weightbearing and balance.

It includes taking weight on:

large body surfaces (front, back, side, hips);
combinations of small body parts (two hands + one foot, two knees + one hand, etc.);
two body parts (hand + foot, knee + foot, hands, etc.);
single body parts (one foot, one hip, head, etc.);
positions where the body is supported below, or to the side of the supporting base (hanging, gripping on apparatus, etc.);
moving into a balance;
moving out of a balance.

Support weight on large body parts

Balance on small body parts

The larger or more numerous the point(s) of support, the easier it is to hold a still position. Balances can only be maintained if the centre of gravity is over the supporting base, unless the performer is very skilled.

Tasks presented should aim to both increase the child's movement vocabulary and improve quality of performance.

Tasks:

1 Balance on many different body parts.
2 Balance on large parts/surfaces.
3 Balance so that there are four points of contact with the floor.
4 Balance so that there are three points of contact with the floor.
5 Balance so that there are two points of contact with the floor.
6 Choose one balance and practise it.
7 Balance and then roll until you can repeat the same balance.
8 Choose one balance and find three different body shapes, keeping the supporting base the same.
9 Link the three variations together using stepping and rolling actions.
10 Roll to finish balanced on four/three/two body parts.
11 Roll, balance and roll out of balance.
12 Jump, land and balance.
13 Jump, land, balance and roll out.
14 Link together one balance on a large body surface, one on four points of contact and one on two or a single point of contact.
15 Choose three balances and link them using a roll, a jump and a spinning action.
16 Choose one balance and perform it three times in a sequence, using a different action each time as a linking movement.

Using benches and mats:

1 Choose three balances you can hold on the floor and perform them on the bench.
2 Find two other balances on the bench.
3 Find ways of balancing so that you are supported partly on the floor and partly on the bench.
4 Balance on the bench, step out of balance and into another balance on the mat.
5 Balance using the floor and the bench, roll out and into a balance on the mat.
6 Travel across mat and into a balance on the floor and the bench.
7 Balance on the bench, travel along the bench, balance on bench and floor and roll into a finishing balance on the mat.

Balance using bench

8 Choose one balance on floor, one balance on bench, one using both bench and floor, and one other, and link them to form a sequence.
9 Turn bench over. Walk along to centre, stop and hold position. Walk to end.
10 Walk half way, half turn and hold position, walk backwards to end.
11 Find other balances on upturned bench.
12 Travel length of upturned bench showing three balances on the way.
13 Stand on upturned bench, jump, land and balance.
14 Run and jump to land in a balance on upturned bench.

On apparatus:

1 Find new balances made possible by the apparatus.
2 Balance so that you are upside down.
3 Balance so that you are hanging from apparatus.
4 Balance so that you are supporting weight by gripping apparatus.
5 Choose two different balances on each piece of apparatus arrangement. Practise them.
6 Link one of the balances on each piece to make a sequence.
7 Choose one balance where you are upside down, one using hands and feet, and one of your choice and link them to make a sequence.
8 Travel to a piece of apparatus and arrive on it in a balanced position.
9 Arrive on apparatus balanced on a combination of hands and one knee or foot.
10 Balance on hands so that apparatus helps you to maintain balance (for example, against box or bars).
11 Balance so that there is one point of contact with the floor and one or two points of contact with the apparatus.
12 Link a balance on hands, a balance on a piece of apparatus and a balance using floor and apparatus to make a sequence.

Specific skills which could be selected for practice by the whole class or particular groups:

On floor

'V' sit;
headstand;
shoulder balance;
arabesque;
handstand;
'Chinese' handstand.

On bench

headstand (head on floor, hands on bench);
headstand (head and hand on floor, other hand on bench);
half lever.

On apparatus

front support on beam;
handstand using apparatus as support;
headstand on apparatus.

4   Taking the weight on the hands

This skill is so fundamental to gymnastics work, that it is suggested that it should be a part of every lesson. It includes:

handstands;
cartwheels;
bridges;
dive rolling activities;
walkovers;
balancing using hands as support (headstand, half lever, planches);
headsprings;
handsprings;
flic flacs;
vaulting activities;
climbing activities;
heaving and pulling activities;
hanging and swinging activities.

In the class teaching situation, the possibilities open to the child working on the floor will be exhausted well before apparatus possibilities are exhausted. Many floor skills involving taking weight on the hands are too advanced or difficult for the average or less able child. Floor work will thus involve practice rather than exploration.

Tasks:

1   Balance so that you use your hands as part of the supporting base.
2   Handstand from single take off (for handstand practices and more related tasks, see section on basic skills).

Balance on hands

3 Handstand from single or double take off.
4 Handstand and come down in a different finishing position.
5 Roll, stand up and handstand.
6 Handstand and roll.
7 Cartwheel (see basic skills for practices and progressions).
8 Begin on feet, take weight onto hands and bring feet down in a different place.
9 Turn round or over so that weight is taken on hands and feet only.
10 Choose one action involving taking weight on hands and add flight onto the hands (for example, dive forward roll, dive cartwheel, dive walkover).

On benches:

1 Balance on bench using hands only, or hands as part of supporting base.
2 Balance with hands on the floor and some other body part on the bench.
3 Balance with hands on the bench and some other body part on the floor.

Balance on hands using apparatus to maintain balance

4 Cross bench taking weight on hands.
5 Cross bench without touching it to take weight on hands on landing side.
6 Cartwheel over bench with hands on bench, on floor, or one on bench and one on floor.

On apparatus:

1 Get onto apparatus taking weight on hands.
2 Get over apparatus taking weight on hands.
3 Get off apparatus taking weight on hands.
4 Get onto apparatus taking weight on hands, travel along and get off taking weight on hands.

Many vaulting activities include taking weight on the hands

5   Get off apparatus by putting your hands on the floor first and taking your weight on them.
6   Balance on your apparatus so that your weight is on your hands.
7   Balance on your apparatus so that you are upside down, supported by your hands.
8   Balance so that you are supporting yourself by gripping or hanging using your hands.
9   Balance so that your hands are on the floor and the apparatus helps you to hold the balance.
10 Balance on or from your apparatus with your weight on your hands. Show three different body shapes with the same balance.
11 Travel along bars using hands only.
12 Travel along bars using hands and feet.
13 Begin on floor and get onto bars taking weight onto hands at some stage.

Most vaulting activities involve taking the weight on the hands and can be taught to some or all of a class. Appropriate support from the teacher must be given where necessary. Children can also be taught to support each other. Decisions as to how much children are to be given the responsibility for this must be made by the individual teacher. The child's capacity for taking responsibility in this way is often underestimated. However, it does depend upon the cultivation of the right kind of working atmosphere and upon the development of the child's ability to take responsibility.

5   Jumping

These activities include:

(a)   different take offs: single; double.

(b)   different landings: to one foot; to other foot; to both feet.

(c)   jumping for height.

(d)   jumping for distance.

(e)   showing different body shapes: tuck; pike; straddle; star; stretched; twisted.

(f)   with turn: quarter; half; full.

(g)   with turn and different take offs and landings.

(h)   onto, off or over apparatus.

Jump forwards, backwards or sideways

(i)　　from springboard or trampette.

(j)　　in using springboard or trampette with apparatus.

Tasks:

1　Jump on spot concentrating on resilient landings.
2　Jump forwards, backwards and sideways with resilient landings.
3　Run, jump and land.

Jumps showing different body shapes in the air

4   Run, jump, land and roll.
5   Jump as high as you can.
6   Jump as far as you can.
7   Jump so that you take off from one foot and land on two.
8   Jump so that you take off from one foot and land on the other.
9   Take off from two feet and land on two feet.
10 Choose a spot on the floor and take off and land on that spot
     (a)   from two feet to two feet,
     (b)   from one foot to two feet.
11 Jump so that you turn in the air.
12 Quarter turn jump and roll sideways.
13 Half turn jump and roll backwards.
14 Full turn jump and roll forwards.
15 Stretch jump, forward roll. Repeat.
16 Half turn jump, land and roll backwards, half turn jump, land and roll forwards.
17 Jump and show a tucked position in the air.
18 Show a different body shape in the air.

19 Jump sideways, taking off from one foot and landing on two feet (use free leg to help jump).
20 Jump showing one body shape, land, roll and jump again showing a different body shape.
21 Jump, land and balance. Roll and jump again using a different take off from the first jump.

Using benches and mats:

1 Run and jump off bench using it as a springboard.
2 Jump off bench showing different body shape.
3 Run along bench and jump from the end aiming for distance.
4 Jump over bench.
5 Jump turning quarter or half staying on bench the whole time.
6 Run and jump off bench using a turning jump.
7 Run half way along bench and jump off sideways.
8 Jump onto bench and jump off.
9 Half turn jump onto bench and jump off backwards.
10 Half turn jump onto bench, half turn jump off.
11 Roll towards bench, into jump to land on bench.
12 Roll along bench into jump staying on bench the whole time.

Using apparatus:

1 Get onto apparatus and jump off.
2 Tuck jump from apparatus.
3 Straddle jump from apparatus.
4 Show other body shapes jumping from apparatus.
5 Jump to catch apparatus (see safety section).
6 Jump over apparatus.
7 Jump off apparatus sideways or backwards.
8 Turning jump from apparatus.
9 Jump to get onto apparatus and roll round or off.
10 Use apparatus in your arrangement to show two different jumps, two different rolls and an action where you take your weight on your hands.
11 Move along apparatus using hands and feet and jump off showing a turn.
12 Get onto apparatus to land still on apparatus.
13 Get onto apparatus and perform a turning jump on apparatus.
14 Get onto apparatus, jump to land still on apparatus and use a rolling action to get off.

It is important that the apparatus chosen is suitable for the tasks set both in type and in height and that mats of an appropriate thickness are positioned as necessary for safety.

6 Partner work

Partner work may be used as a development of work on other topics, or as an area of work in its own right. Partner work may be with or without contact with the partner. The latter clearly demands greater co-operation and interdependence and will generally involve more advanced work because of this.

Partner work may include:

matching and mirroring partner's actions;
different relationships to partner (side by side/facing/back to back, etc.);
meeting and parting;
assisted balance – one active, one passive/one base one supporter/both active, i.e. counterbalance, countertension.

For some partner work, partners should be of fairly similar height and weight.

Tasks:

1 Follow partner about gym keeping about three feet behind.
2 Ditto, partner changing direction.

Balances that both partners can perform

Balances that both partners can perform

3 Face partner – one mirror the action of the other.
4 Follow partner, copying partner's action.
5 Follow partner, front person make barrier for partner to jump over. New front person repeat.
6 Move side by side trying to copy exactly.

Using mats:

1 Perform any movement so that you copy partner exactly, starting side by side and synchronising actions.
2 Ditto but start opposite partner.
3 Ditto but start back to back.
4 Ditto starting side by side but facing opposite directions.

One balance so that partner can get over

5 Find two more actions that you can both perform and perform these as in 1–4 above.
6 Make up a sequence including forward roll, turning jump and one other action and teach it to your partner.
7 Repeat 1–4 but one follow the other instead of moving simultaneously.
8 Find balances that both partners can perform.
9 Make up a sequence linking three different balances and teach it to your partner so that you can both perform the sequence in unison.
10 Make up a sequence of four balances with linking actions and perform it so that you and your partner alternate moving one at a time and moving in unison.
11 One balance so that partner can jump over.
12 One balance so that partner can get over or under in other ways (without contact).
13 One balance showing a large or small body shape. Partner show a similar body shape when negotiating obstacle.
14 Ditto but show a contrasting body shape.

Balance showing counterbalance

Balance showing countertension

One support partner's weight

15 After negotiating partner, find a balance so that partner can get over you (without contact).
16 Work out a sequence of three balances each so that you alternately balance and get over partner's balance.
17 One help partner to hold a balance which she could not maintain alone.
18 One support partner's weight so that she can hold balance.
19 Balance so that both partners play an equal part (counterbalance or countertension).
20 Travel to partner, balance together and travel away from each other.

Using apparatus:

1 Follow partner onto and off apparatus, copying actions.
2 Get onto and off apparatus from different starting points to arrive on apparatus at the same time.
3 Travel to apparatus from different starting points to arrive on apparatus at the same time.
4 Ditto and travel away from apparatus in a different direction.

5 Approach from different directions, negotiate apparatus at same time as partner and travel away.
6 Follow partner onto apparatus and both get off together using same action.
7 Ditto but showing contrasting body shapes.
8 Travel onto apparatus and show identical balances before getting off.
9 One balance on apparatus so that partner can get over or under.
10 Find balances on apparatus using counterbalance or countertension.
11 Find balances where one partner supports the other.
12 Work out a sequence on apparatus travelling to balance together then moving away again, repeating this pattern to form a sequence.

4 *The core skills of gymnastics*

The teaching of gymnastics skills is frequently equated with a direct class activity approach to the subject and rejected as an educational experience because of the high skill threshold of many gymnastics actions. There are, however, a number of core skills which arise in gymnastics work, whatever approach is adopted, and which may be practised with benefit by a whole class.

Reference has been made in the two previous chapters to a number of specific skills which might be included or which might be expected to appear in work with a particular focus. This chapter looks at these core skills, at the teaching points which should be considered, at common faults which may be found and at progressions and variations which will be needed in order to continue to provide a challenge for a mixed ability class.

The place of the teaching of specific skills is considered in Chapter 6 when the provision of a balanced programme is discussed.

1 Forward roll

Teaching points:

crouch start;
hands flat on floor, about shoulder width apart, fingers forward;
push with legs, tuck head well in;
keep tucked, round back;
put feet on floor close to hips, reach forward and up with arms;
when weight is on balls of feet, stand up.

Common faults:

head not tucked in – discomfort in roll;
back not rounded – discomfort in roll;

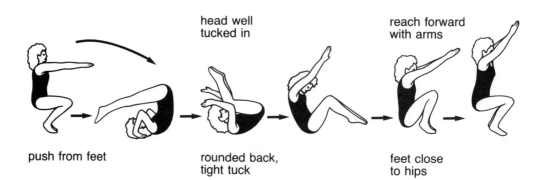

head well
tucked in

reach forward
with arms

push from feet

rounded back,
tight tuck

feet close
to hips

Figure 4.1 Forward roll

hands incorrectly placed – failure to stand up or failure with later skills;
feet too far away from hips – failure to stand up;
uneven push from hands – crooked roll;
head turned sideways – crooked roll;
insufficient push from legs – failure to roll.

Progressions:

rolling to different finishing positions (see work cards, Chapter 8);
rolling from different starting positions (see work cards);
dive forward roll;
rolling off apparatus;
rolling on apparatus, for example, along benches, flat surfaces;
rolling onto apparatus, for example, onto boxes or other flat surfaces;
rolling round beams, bars.

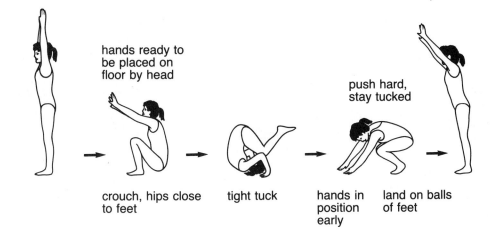

hands ready to
be placed on
floor by head

push hard,
stay tucked

crouch, hips close
to feet

tight tuck

hands in
position
early

land on balls
of feet

Figure 4.2 Backward roll

2   Backward roll

Teaching points:

crouch start;
hands in position early, flat on floor close to head, thumbs point towards
ears;
tuck tightly, knees onto chest;
push hard from hands, stay tucked;
maintain push and land on balls of feet.

Common faults:

lack of momentum – unable to complete roll;
hands incorrectly placed – unable to push;
uneven push from hands – crooked roll;
opening out too soon – unable to get to feet, or to get over at all.

Progressions:

rolling to different starting positions;
rolling to different finishing positions;
rolling on apparatus;
rolling off apparatus, for example, box, beam;
back roll through handstand.

Practices for rolling:

rocking to and fro, staying tucked and building momentum;
rolling on a slightly inclined surface;
rolling between ropes;
rolling from box (forwards).

---

3   Headstand

Teaching points:

head and hands in triangle on floor;
forehead on floor;
walk feet up towards hands, on toes;
push down with hands and lift feet into tucked headstand;
keep back straight;
straighten legs.

Common faults:

head and hands in line on floor – overbalance;
back of head on floor – overbalance;
straightening legs too soon – failure to invert;
straightening legs when off balance – collapse of headstand;
back not straight – collapse of headstand.

Practices:

against wall;
off end of box;
to hook knees over bar at appropriate height;
with support.

walk feet up
towards hands,
on toes

head and hands
in triangle,
push on hands,
lift feet off floor

straight back,
balance before
trying to straighten
legs

Figure 4.3 Headstand

Progressions:

from different starts;
to different finishes;
with straight legs throughout;
from lying flat on front;
off apparatus;
on flat surfaces;
off apparatus.

4   Handstand

Teaching points:

hands shoulder width apart;
fingers face forward;
eyes look at hands;
arms straight;
hips over shoulders;
body straight.

Figure 4.4 Handstand

Common faults:

hands too far apart – handstand collapses;
arms bent – handstand collapses;
head looking too far forward – hyper-extension in spine or inability to invert;
back arching instead of straight – weak position.

Practices:

'kicking horses';
hands on floor, walk feet up wall or wallbars;
with support;
against wall;
from box.

Progressions:

from different starts;
to different finishes;
from two-footed take off;
from two-footed take off with legs straight;
off apparatus;
over apparatus.

Figure 4.5 Cartwheel

5   Cartwheel

Teaching points:

face forward to start;
chest towards knee of bent leg;
push hard from bent leg, swing other leg up;
wide straddle;
arms straight;
head look at floor;
body straight;
put first foot close to hands, eyes looking at hand on floor;
hands and feet should contact floor in a straight line.

Common faults:

incorrect sequence of hands and feet;
poor body position;
legs not lifted over shoulders.

Practices:

Use chalk marks on floor to practise correct sequence of hands and feet – this is essential before body position, etc. can be improved.

Progressions:

> from different starts;
> with flight;
> using one hand only;
> along flat surface, for example, box or bench;
> over apparatus;
> several cartwheels in succession;
> cartwheel in either direction.

6   Headspring

Teaching points:

> hips lead body off balance;
> strong swing from straight legs;
> extension of hips to arch back;
> strong push from hands;
> push hips forward to land on balls of feet.

Common faults:

> poor timing, usually early push – insufficient rotation;
> lack of hip extension, bent legs;
> insufficient push from hands – failure to get to feet;
> excessive arching of back – over rotation;
> lack of body tension – collapsing.

This skill should be taught with support.
The performer must be able to perform a competent headstand with legs straight.
Many children who find it difficult to generate sufficient push from the floor can learn this skill as a vault.

Figure 4.6 Headspring

---

7   Handspring

Teaching points:

hurdle step preparation – long and low;
shoulders extended, chest towards floor;
strong leg kick, arms straight, shoulders behind hands;
strong push from hands/shoulders, legs come together;
keep body straight, hips forward;
land on balls of feet.

Common faults:

hands placed on floor close to feet instead of reaching forward;
bending arms;
lack of body tension causing poor body position with insufficient extension;
push from shoulders at wrong time;
tucking or collapsing into landing leading to pitching forward.

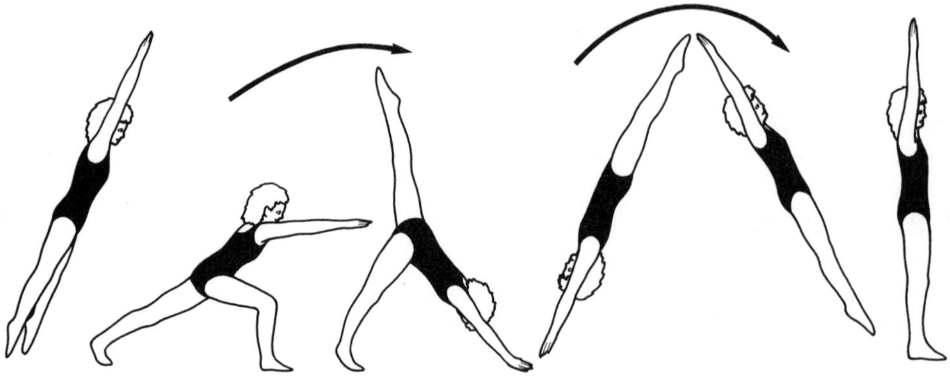

Figure 4.7 Handspring

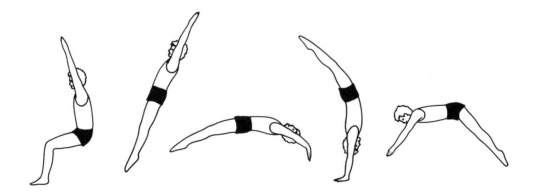

Figure 4.8 Flic flac

The gymnast must be able to perform a good handstand before attempting this skill.
It should be learned with support.

8   Flic flac

Teaching points:

push on take off through heels not balls of feet;
knees should be behind feet;
strong push from feet;
arms swing forward and up over head;
head in line with body;
body extended but not excessively so;
legs together and straight;
body should pass through handstand;
bring feet down together.

Common faults:

incorrect angle of take off, drive from toes or balls of feet instead of heels;
drive taking body high rather than along – flic flac should be long and low;
arms not in position for landing;
tucking legs up or failing to keep legs together.

This move must be taught with support.

5 Teaching styles and techniques

This chapter looks at aspects of lesson presentation in the context of gymnastics teaching. The first section discusses teaching styles, and the second focuses on a selection of specific techniques needed whatever style is used and which would be equally relevant to the teaching of activities other than gymnastics.

An examination of educational documents, reports and syllabuses reveals changes in advocated styles of teaching or method of presentation. These reflect alterations over this century in the aims and purposes of education. The aims of physical education, like those of education as a whole, have changed and increased in scope since the early days of universal education. The philosophies which underpin the the continued inclusion of gymnastics in the curriculum, discussed in Chapter 1, suggest that gymnastics may contribute to the achievement of a number of the aims of education and physical education. In order to do so, a number of teaching styles may be needed. The following section looks at some of these.

Styles of teaching

Variety in the method of presentation is a key feature of modern gymnastics teaching if it is accepted that gymnastics should be seen as a means to the achievement of aims in a number of areas of experience. A range of teaching styles are recognised and accepted as having value, although in practice it appears that much teaching remains didactic and teacher-dominated. Public examinations are frequently blamed for the tendency to rely excessively upon direct teaching methods in other subject areas. It could be argued that too close an alliance with coaching will produce a similar lack of variety in physical education because of the coach's concern with physical skill as the overriding priority.

Styles of teaching are generally categorised according to the extent to which pupils are given a choice of response. Earlier this century, physical education syllabuses gave no freedom of choice to the pupil, and little to the teacher, who was expected to follow the tables of exercises prescribed. These gave precise guidelines not only on the movements required, but also on the instructions which were to be given by the teacher.

The change in philosophy towards a more 'child-centred' approach to education led to changes in methods of presentation. 'Traditional work', implying teacher-dominated lessons with a strong element of discipline and obedience training, was contrasted with more 'modern' approaches which encouraged the child to think for himself and to work out his own solution to problems set. Kane's survey of physical education in the secondary school questioned teachers on their use of five teaching 'styles': direct, guided discovery, problem-solving, individualised learning and creative, although no definition of the various styles was offered.

Teaching style may be seen as a continuum with completely closed, teacher-directed approaches at one extreme and very open-ended approaches at the other. Increasing the amount of pupil choice may be seen as contributing to individuality of response and to creativity. Mosston (1981) takes the relationship between teaching style and pupil performance further by providing a framework for understanding how style of teaching may affect progress in the various aspects of development which could be said to be relevant to the physical education teacher. Mosston suggests that the teacher can select from a 'spectrum' of styles, in which, at one extreme, the teacher makes all the decisions with the pupil playing a completely passive role. At the other end of the continuum the pupil makes all the decisions with the teacher acting as facilitator. The range of styles in between the two extremes reflects various shifts in the decision-making process which gradually increase the involvement of the pupil.

Mosston suggests that while the 'command' style of teaching in which the teacher is dominant may achieve significant progress in the areas of physical development, this may well be at the expense of development in emotion and intellectual areas. This style would therefore be inappropriate as a single teaching method in a system which seeks to promote aspects of development other than the purely physical. Mosston seeks to encourage the use of alternative styles in order to increase the active involvement of the student in the learning process, thereby enabling him to make progress in emotional, social and intellectual as well as physical development. Such an approach appears to be consistent with the emphasis currently being placed upon the personal and social development of the child, and with the need for intelligent performance rather than the rote repetition of skills.

While there is still a place for teaching skills to the whole class and for direct teaching of certain procedures, there is also a need to create situations which allow for a variety of response and which encourage the child to make decisions and to apply knowledge and understanding. Use of a variety of teaching methods should give all pupils opportunities for satisfaction and success and should develop understanding and appreciation as well as specific skills and agilities.

Different teaching styles in practice

Examples of tasks which might be set within various styles of presentation are given below. Some indication of the merits and limitations of each style is offered. The styles follow the principles suggested by Mosston but are not identical.

1 Teaching by command

The teacher is dominant. He dictates not only the exact nature of the activity but also when the pupils should begin and when they should stop the activity. The pupil's role is to try to attain the standards of performance demanded by the teacher. He does so by obeying instructions and doing as he is told without question. The use of this style of presentation will produce uniformity, conformity, quick response to instructions and adherence to a specific perform-ance model which may be demonstrated by the teacher.

Early syllabuses of PT provide excellent examples of this style of teaching. While relevant in some situations, this style makes no allowance for individual differences, and, by denying the pupil an active role in the learning process, minimises opportunities for other than physical development. Even physical development may be hampered because some children will be held back to the level of others while the lowest ability child may fail to achieve anything at all.

'Balance on your shoulders, roll back to your feet and jump. Land and balance on your shoulders again, roll back to your feet and jump ...'

'Head and hands in a triangle, lift into a headstand, point your toes, and come back down and back onto your feet.'

'Forward rolls down the mats, wait at the other end when you get there – GO.'

'Through vaults, strong push, land and hold it. Next, strong push, land and stand still. Next ...'

2 Teaching through practice

Here, while the teacher still dictates the activity, the pupil practises in his own time. He now make decisions about when to stop and when to begin. If mats and apparatus are being shared, some co-operation is required. The teacher can now offer feedback to individuals, thereby beginning to cater for individual differences, although the limitations placed upon the activity mean that a number of children will be ready for a new task while others have not mastered the first activity.

'Practise headstands. Remember to put your head and hands in a triangle on the floor. Off you go.'

'I want to see you working on forward rolls, concentrating particularly on the finish of the roll.'

'A few steps, double take off, ½ turn jump, land and roll backwards. Practise on your mat.'

3 Reciprocal teaching

Reciprocal teaching involves working in pairs. By utilising pupils to provide feedback, one of the difficulties faced by the teacher of a large group is overcome. In addition to the assistance given to the active partner, the pupil who adopts the teaching role may derive many benefits in terms of personal and social development and through increased understanding which may also be acquired. Co-operative behaviour is obviously required. This style may be utilised at many levels of pupil choice. The teacher may continue to dictate the activity and may use partners solely for providing feedback. Alternatively, a freer choice may be given to either partner in the selection of the activity.

'One of you watch the other's handstand and check that his hands are in the right place, his head is looking at the floor and his legs are straight.'

'Look at your partner's sequence and see whether you can help him to improve it.'

'Most of your balances look very untidy. Watch your partner and tell him how he could improve.'

'Take a work card, look at the pictures and the list of things to look for then teach your partner to do the actions on the card.'

4 Teaching through limitation

Here pupils are given options within the task set which enable the teacher to cater for individual differences within the class. The pupil has to make decisions concerning the appropriate option relative to his ability. The teacher continues to direct the pupils towards specific activities.

'Choose either a headstand or a shoulder balance or a handstand and practise it.'

'Now finish your roll either in a straddle position or on two knees.'

'Practise headstands either with your legs tucked, or going from a tuck to straight legs, or lifting up with your legs straight throughout.'

'Use handstand forward roll either to get off your apparatus or to get onto and along it.'

'Choose a jump, a roll and a balance and join them together.'

5 Guided discovery

This style is the first to offer the learner greater choice and the opportunity to create his own response or to discover the solution to a task for himself. The teacher may follow the tasks given below with others which can lead the pupil towards the discovery of a predetermined end. This style may be used to guide pupils to make their own decisions as to the most effective way of performing particular skills or to guide pupils towards trying particular groups of activities.

'Balance on two hands and two feet then balance on one foot. Which is easier? Why?'

'Look at where the head and hands are placed in these demonstrations. Which do you think makes the most stable base? Why?'

'Get onto the box so that you take your weight on your hands.'

'Get over the horse so that you land facing a different way.'

6 Divergent thinking or problem-solving

This style like guided discovery, encourages the pupil to seek solutions for himself, but unlike guided discovery, where the teacher guides the pupil towards a predetermined end, this style encourages creativity on the part of the pupil and invites him to discover alternative solutions.

'How many balances can you find which use three points of contact with the floor?'

'How else can you finish a forward roll?'

'How can you come out of a handstand?'

'How can you get over your apparatus so that you turn upside down?'

It can be seen from the examples given that the method of presentation selected will produce a particular style of teaching which will in turn affect the behaviour of the learner and the outcome of the lesson. To suggest that one style is 'better' than another is to misunderstand the nature of the relationship between teaching style and learning outcome, and to fail to appreciate that one style might produce results in the area of social or moral development, while another may be more effective in facilitating physical development. The appropriate style, therefore, depends upon the teacher's philosophy, aims and priorities. The greater the range of styles which the teacher can call upon, the better his chances of influencing pupil development in a variety of areas.

It should also be remembered that pupils have to acquire the facility to work in particular ways, and that their initial reaction to an unfamiliar approach from the teacher may well be unfavourable, especially if the approach differs radically from that to which they are accustomed. The teacher must therefore be prepared to persevere and to make gradual progress towards achieving the kind of relationship which he wishes to attain with his class.

It is also fair to say that the inexperienced teacher often feels more at ease with the structured situation offered by a more direct approach. It is, however, important to master the more difficult technique of ensuring that all children work constructively in the freer atmosphere which arises with less didactic approaches.

Teaching techniques

One of the features of gymnastics in the curriculum should be that it offers opportunities for using varied teaching methods, from open-ended tasks in order to foster individuality and promote thoughtful application to solve problems, to closed tasks set by the teacher in order to improve specific skills or improve quality of performance or increase physical capacity.

Whichever general approach is adopted, the teacher will need to select appropriate teaching techniques to reinforce what is wanted and to eliminate the irrelevant. Several different approaches will often be needed in order to make progress to the desired result. These techniques include the use of observation, demonstration and of questioning.

Observation

The ability to observe and to react to what is seen is *absolutely fundamental to good teaching*. This ability is particularly important where a whole class is working at the same time, producing varied responses to the task set. If the teacher's powers of observation are inadequate, he will be unable to use and develop the work which is being produced.

Observation once work has begun can serve a number of purposes. The inexperienced teacher finds it difficult to take in all that is happening and needs to decide what is being looked for, gradually extending this as powers of observation develop. It should be remembered that observation improves with practice and that what was initially a conscious effort on the part of the teacher will, in time, become automatic, enabling him to concentrate on other aspects of the lesson.

Suggested procedure for observing and reacting to what is seen

1 Is the class working safely?

There is a clear relation between safety and observation by the teacher. While most children tend to avoid attempting tasks beyond their abilities, they may unwittingly be encouraged to do so by peer group pressure or by suggestion by the teacher. In particular, young children are generally trusting and more likely to believe the teacher who tells them that it will be safe for them to try something.

When apparatus is being moved then the teacher's ability to observe and notice whether equipment is being carried correctly and safely set up, whether instructions are being followed and so on, is crucial in avoiding dangerous situations.

Action by teacher   Stop class and make sure that they appreciate the need to ask for help before attempting potentially dangerous skills and to ask the teacher if they have any doubts about the safety of what they wish to attempt.

Follow procedures in section on organisation and handling of apparatus (see p.91). *Insist that instructions are followed.*

2 Is the class answering the task set?

The teacher must ask this before progressing to anything else. If the task is not being answered by everyone, is this because:
(a)   children have not listened;
(b)   there is genuine misunderstanding;
(c)   the task is simply too difficult or otherwise inappropriate?

Action by teacher   Repeat the task. Speak to one or two individuals. Clarify the task further for the whole class. Modify the task in some way.

3 How well is the task being answered?

(a)   Is a variety of response being sought? If so, are the ideas being introduced relevant to the task set, and are the range of movements being produced adequate?
(b)   Is quality of performance being sought through teaching a specific skill or giving the opportunity to practise a selection of actions?

4 Which aspects of work need improvement?

The teacher must be able to answer this question in order to offer constructive criticism.

Action by teacher Select the most relevant points and focus attention on these by use of
(a) demonstration and appropriate questions;
(b) repetition of key words;
(c) practice of specific aspects of movement.

5 *Is there some work which could be shown to the rest of the class?*

In selecting work for others to watch, the teacher will be giving an indication of standards. Therefore, what is shown should contain something of value. Observation with a view to selecting work to be shown requires the ability to watch and select from the whole class. Poor observation leads to an inability to extract anything of value from a mass of activity or to looking only at those children from whom good work can generally be expected. Precisely what will be looked for will depend on the purpose of the demonstration.

Action by teacher Tell the pupil that he will be asked to demonstrate and make sure that he knows exactly what is wanted. This is particularly important where pupils are producing a variety of responses to a task and the teacher wants one specific idea shown.

6 *Are individuals working to their capacity?*

Inevitably, much observation is concerned with the class or with groups of children, but the teacher should take every opportunity to observe individuals. By doing this over a period of time, a picture of each child is built up. The teacher is then in a position to both push the able, skilled child, or the able, lazy child, to help the nervous child who lacks confidence or to check the foolhardy.

Action by teacher Give additional instruction which will encourage the able to either extend the difficulty of their response, or to extend their range of response. Suggest simpler alternatives for those who are struggling with movements which are too difficult for them or progressions to help them to build up to mastery of a specific skill.

Demonstration

A good demonstration is an invaluable teaching aid. A bad demonstration is worse than none at all.
    The demonstration may be by: (a) an individual, (b) several individuals, (c) part of the class, for example, half, (d) the teacher.

Organisation of demonstrations

1 Can the whole class see?

It may be necessary to move those watching so that everyone can see, either so that the view is not obscured by apparatus, or so that everyone has a particular view of what is being shown, for example, to the side of a demonstration of a headspring so that the angle of the legs can be seen.

It may be necessary to repeat a demonstration a number of times.

2 Do the children demonstrating know what they are required to do?

This is especially important when they have produced several answers to a task or when the teacher wants a child to emphasise or exaggerate a specific point.

3 What are the observers supposed to look for?

The class needs to be given specific guidelines so that they can gain maximum benefit from watching, for example:

'Watch the other half of the class and choose two that you think are particularly good at showing different body shapes.'

'Watch these balances and see if you can see why they are able to hold the balance so well.'

'Look at these examples of turning and tell me which axis each one turns around.'

'Watch this headstand and tell me exactly where the head and hands are placed.'

Where the teacher wishes to focus the class's attention on particular teaching points, it is important to talk through the demonstration to reinforce these.

Purposes of demonstrations

1 To show a technical point

This can range from how to position the head and hands in a headstand, how to achieve a resilient landing, how to use a springboard, how to operate the wheeling mechanism on a box, or how to take out a set of bars.

These are probably best demonstrated by the teacher where possible, since he should know exactly what is required. What must be given is an impression of what *is* wanted, not one of faults. Half-hearted demonstrations will do more harm than good.

Where a class is working on a skill and a demonstration of a technical point is needed, the teacher should ensure that what is demonstrated will actually prove helpful. This also applies to the extra-curricular club situation. If what is needed is a demonstration of the placing of the hands and the arm movement needed to perform a handspring on the floor, then this should be shown rather than a spectacular performance of the whole skill (although there is, of course, a place for showing children complete skills). Children can be intimidated and classes put off by a demonstration of something apparently well beyond their level of attainment if such a demonstration is given at an inappropriate time.

2   To show something well done

Where the teacher is working to improve quality of performance, a demonstration of this type may be used to illustrate the standard expected. The level of skill is not relevant here but the way in which it is performed is vital. It can therefore be a good opportunity to pick a child whose ability in terms of technical skill is low, but who can show good poise and finish. Individuals may be chosen to show such points as good body tension, extension of legs, 'finish' or a short sequence performed with control and finesse including a good starting and finishing position.

3   To show a range of possibilties

This kind of demonstration is useful when exploratory work has been carried out and can very easily involve a number of children of varying abilities. Alternatively, half the class could show their ideas while the other half watch to see how many different ideas they can identify. For example, while half the class can show a variety of balances, the other half watch to be asked afterwards what different balances they have seen.

4   To compare different aspects of a piece of work

Here two individuals could show contrasting ways of answering a task possibly showing answers suited to different abilities, such as balance on the head with the legs remaining tucked, compared with the same balance where the legs are in a splits position. Alternatively, different answers to a task could be compared to show contrasting possibilties. A task of travelling up an inclined form and getting over the top bar of double bars might be answered by running up the form and vaulting over the top, or by sliding up the form followed by a slow roll over the bar, showing differences in speed and dynamics.

5   To explain a particular concept and establish its features

Here the teacher would choose examples of different categories of activity and use the demonstrations either with questions or with an explanation. A task of finding examples of turning over or round could be followed by a selection of an example of a turn round each of the three body axes: longitudinal, side to side, front to back. These could be a turning jump, a forward roll, and a spinning movement on the stomach. The teacher could then question the class to see whether they knew what an axis was, explaining if necessary, and pointing out the way each example showed a turn round a different axis.

6   To emphasise particular teaching points

Where concentration on a particular aspect of movement is required, a demonstration can be used to reinforce the points which the teacher has been making verbally, or is about to make. When a sequence is being worked out showing a change of speed, the teacher might wish to show an example of a child who was showing the change of speed very clearly, even if other aspects of the sequence still needed further practice. The attention of the class would be focused on the aspect of the work being stressed. Where children were having difficulty standing up after a forward roll because the feet were not being placed sufficiently close to the hips, a demonstration by the teacher to emphasise this point, or by a child showing the correct technique could be used.

7   To stimulate more ambitious movement

This would obviously need to be used with discretion, as one would not wish to stimulate large numbers of children into attempting potentially hazardous skills. Nevertheless, where children are offering an easy solution when capable of more challenging ones, then examples could be shown to encourage them to attempt something more difficult. A forward roll to straddle could be demonstrated for those who found forward roll to standing easy to perform well. A handstand with a two foot take off could also be shown as a challenge to those who were not stretched by simply kicking up into a handstand.

8   To show a fault or faults

Children should *not* be picked out to show how not to do something. It would be quite wrong to use an incompetent child for this purpose and the child who is simply not trying can be dealt with in other ways. There may, however, be occasions when the child can show a movement incorrectly and then correctly performed. Better still, the teacher can show a common fault, exaggerating it as necessary, to show the class what is wrong. This should be followed by a demonstration of the movement as it should be performed.

9   To show completed work

Knowing that they may be asked to show the results of their labours will stimulate some children to greater effort. This kind of demonstration should be by groups rather than individuals. It may be half the class at a time for floor work, or perhaps each group in turn, or two groups at a time on large apparatus.

10   To show something original or otherwise outstanding

There are occasions when someone, or a group, produces a different idea worth showing simply for its originality. There are also times when a class has an exceptionally able child who can provide answers to tasks which would be beyond the reach of other children but which would nevertheless interest them. While it would be unwise to encourage a conceited or otherwise unpopular child to show skills in this situation, another child could well show, for example, flic flacs into somersaults which the class could enjoy watching at close quarters and which could be an appropriate response to the task set.

Children should, whenever possible, be given the opportunity to apply the knowledge which has been acquired through watching a demonstration *immediately* following the demonstration. Much of the purpose of most demonstrations is lost if children do not have the chance to go back and try to put what they have seen into action.

Concentration is necessary on the part of the observers if maximum benefit is to be gained from a demonstration. Children, therefore, need to be trained to watch and to concentrate.

Question and answer

The technique of asking appropriate questions is fundamental to good teaching of any activity, especially where the development of understanding as well as physical skill is required. Questions may serve a number of purposes.

1   To keep attention

If a class expects to be asked questions about a demonstration or explanation then their concentration may well be improved.

2   To emphasise particular teaching points

'Where does Jane put her feet so that she can stand up at the end of her roll?'

'How far apart are Peter's hands in his handstand?'

3   To provoke thought and promote mental activity

'Why do you think Mary is managing to jump so high?'

'How many ways can you think of of balancing on your hands and your feet?'

'Can you think of a different finishing position?'

4   To consolidate knowledge

'What shape do your head and hands make when you do a headstand?'

'What has been helping you to land lightly?'

5   To assist the child's observation and thereby increase understanding

'Watch Jane. How does she use her arms to help her to keep her balance?'

'Look at Sally's headstand. Where are her hips in relation to her shoulders?'

6   To motivate and stimulate

'Can you jump any higher?'

'Can you think of any other answers?'

'Can you make your legs even straighter?'

7   To obtain feedback

Questions may be used to determine ability, understanding, recall, skill level, and so on.

'What balances did we practice last lesson which had two points of support?'

'What were we trying to do with our headstands last week?'

'Why were some balances easier to hold than others?'

8   To involve the class by eliciting information, explanation and application of knowledge

The teacher of gymnastics will ask questions which may be answered in movement as well as ones which require a verbal answer. A balance should be maintained between the two.

   Whatever purpose the question is to serve, a number of points need to be remembered:

1   Question wording should be clear and precise and appropriate to the age and ability of the class. A vague and imprecise question such as, 'What about your arms' gives the child little chance of constructing a reasonable answer.

2   Questions should be ordered in a logical and meaningful way.

3   Ask the question before naming the pupil who is to answer. If the pupil is named first, the rest of the class have no need to think of an answer.

4 Give the class time to answer especially if the question is complex. A common fault among teachers who are inexperienced or who lack confidence is to panic and answer the question for the class who very soon learn that there is no need for them to make any effort because if they wait the teacher will answer for them.

6 | *Lesson structure and progression*

This chapter looks at lesson planning and structure. It also discusses indicators of progress and offers some suggestions as to how improvement in work might be attained.

Lesson structure

The following format is suggested unless particular circumstances (such as are discussed later) prohibit its adoption.

1 Warm up/introduction

This should provide both physical and mental preparation for the lesson. Wherever practicable, children should be encouraged to enter the gymnasium and begin working purposefully as soon as they are changed so that valuable working time is not wasted. In an ideal situation one might expect a whole class to warm up independently of the teacher. However, this may well be unrealistic, in which case a teacher-directed warm up should ensure that all are prepared and ready to go on to the next phase of the lesson.

In some conditions this part of the lesson may be needed to physically warm the body. Limbering will always be needed. Younger children may require energetic movement to remove surplus energy so that they are ready to concentrate on the task in hand. Older children may need a slower introduction until they are mentally attuned to the idea of physical activity.

Whole body activities should be included followed by flexibility and mobility exercises involving large muscle groups. Since this part of the lesson will set the tone for what is to follow, it is important that activities selected have a 'gymnastics orientation' and demand standards of work appropriate to gymnastics. Children should also understand the purpose of warming and limbering up for gymnastics as for other physical activities.

The need for mental preparation should not be ignored. In other lessons the focus is unlikely to be on movement. Therefore, a time at the beginning of the lesson is necessary for a transition to be made from the challenges presented in the classroom to those presented in an activity lesson.

2 Movement training/individual work/small apparatus work

The main emphasis of the lesson is introduced and developed. The aim is two-fold:

(a)   to explore the possibilities within an area so that each child is aware of the choices open to her and to others, and can thus extend her personal vocabulary of movement;

(b)   to improve skill and extend movement knowledge and understanding so that each member of the class learns to perform as well as her individual abilities allow. This requires practice of skills. Certain basics may be taught to the whole class. Beyond this level a degree of choice will be needed if all are to be purposefully employed.

Some work may be usefully covered using the floor space only. However, for many activities mats will be needed if discomfort is not to limit the range of possible movements. There may be times where other small apparatus such as benches, planks, box tops, may also be useful.

3. Large apparatus/group work

Work covered in the previous part of the lesson or in earlier lessons is applied to the new situation created by the introduction of apparatus. Work on apparatus, like work on the floor, has a two-fold aim:

(a)   to discover the range of possibilities open to the child on various pieces of apparatus. Many activities attempted on the floor may be transferred onto large apparatus. Some will be facilitated by the use of apparatus, for example, taking the weight on the hands where the apparatus may provide a support. Others will be more challenging, for example, a headstand on a high box or a forward roll along a box or plank. In addition, apparatus opens up a whole new range of possibilities especially in hanging, gripping or swinging activities;

(b)   to improve skill and attain high quality performance.

4 Conclusion

When the apparatus has been put away, a task should be set to round off the lesson. It should be a calming down period, ready for return to the classroom.

The proportion of time allocated to each part of the lesson should be considered at the preparation stage. In the early stages of a block of work, more time will probably be given to floor work, with proportionately less time on large apparatus. As work progresses, the time allocation will change until towards the end of a block of lessons, the majority of the lesson will be devoted to large apparatus work. By this stage an area of work should have been fully explored on the floor.

For various reasons, the above outline may vary. In some schools, single lessons may be so short that attempting to include both floor and apparatus work in each lesson will be counterproductive if not impossible. Nothing worthwhile will be achieved. In these cases it may be necessary to devote one lesson to floor work and the next to apparatus work. The balance of floor to apparatus lessons will depend upon the work being undertaken. In the apparatus lesson the warm up should be slightly extended to include a recap of the work done the previous lesson so that the link between floor work and apparatus work is retained. If double lessons can be timetabled these are usually preferable. Another possibility is to share a block of three lessons with another subject.

With some classes it may be advisable to spend the whole of the first lesson of a new block of work on the floor or using only small apparatus. In this way the the particular aims of the lesson and the desired teaching points may be reinforced better than by the immediate introduction of large apparatus. The end result may well be better because it is based on firmer foundations than would be possible if the establishment of a new idea or group of skills were to be rushed simply for the sake of completing a 'whole' lesson. There are also times, especially in partner or group work, where classes become involved with working without apparatus, and where the teacher might wish to capitalise on their involvement rather than break their concentration by getting apparatus out.

Planning for a 'balanced' experience

The question of how to offer a balanced programme both within a lesson and over a series of lessons should be considered when planning. A number of factors should be considered.

1   Is there a balance between 'doing' and 'thinking'? Gymnastics should involve 'doing with understanding' and the development of intelligent performance (in common with other activities in physical education). Some thought and discussion should be directed to increasing the pupil's understanding and knowledge in order to produce intelligent performance

at all levels of technical expertise. It should also be remembered, however, that gymnastics can also be a means of body training and of increasing strength, stamina and flexibility. This demands vigorous physical activity which should not be totally sacrificed to rather aimless debate about work being done.

2   Is there a balance between development of skill and high quality performance and increasing the variety and range of movement?

Skill development and refinement of technique cannot take place unless there is opportunity for repetition and practice. A very small degree of open-endedness is all that is required to cater for individual differences. Within this, pupils should frequently select a pattern of movement and practise it otherwise progression will not take place.

Range of movement is equally unlikely to be increased through the setting of very open-ended tasks, since many pupils will simply repeat those movements with which they are already familiar. Tightly constrained tasks are needed which demand alternative responses. Whether these are dictated by the teacher or left to the child to choose, is a decision to be made by the teacher.

3   Is there a balanced allocation of time? The body should be properly prepared through warming and limbering activities. Time should be divided appropriately between floor and apparatus.

4   Are tasks organised so that there is balance in the demands made of the body, so that actions include use of (a) feet alone, (b) hands and feet, or hands alone, (c) large body surfaces?

5   Are both fast dynamic movements and slower more sustained movements demanded in all lessons?

6   Is apparatus planned to give a balanced range of activities, i.e. hanging, circling, heaving, vaulting, rolling, etc?

7   Is the apparatus organised so that apparatus changes involve a change of type of activity?

This may mean a change from an activity which makes demands on the upper body (such as hanging, heaving) to one which makes a different kind of demand (such as springing, or rolling), or a change from a single piece of apparatus requiring the practice of particular activities, to an arrangement which demands the linking together or a number of different movements.

8   Is there a balance between teacher directed activities and those which allow the pupil some degree of choice?

9   Is there a balance between the practice and performance of individual skills, and the construction of sequences of actions?

10 Is the work on body action supported by an appropriate emphasis on spatial and dynamic aspects of gymnastics?

Progression in gymnastics

If gymnastics is to be a successful part of the physical education curriculum, there must be progression both within a block of work and from theme to theme.

Progression within a series of lessons

1 Has the child extended her movement repertoire by adding more actions or short movement phrases?

To achieve this, tasks must be set where limitations encourage the pupil to widen her movement vocabulary by adding actions/skills of a similar difficulty to those already mastered, for example, having learned a forward roll to stand, other finishing positions should be mastered such as on one leg, on one knee or two knees, lying flat, long sitting and so on. Other basic skills may be extended in the same way. This implies not only developing skill in body management but also developing the pupil's ability to think.

2 Has the child learned new skills, actions or sequences which are technically more difficult for that child?

This will also be achieved by setting limited tasks. Constraints will be more exacting and a specific line of progression may be required so that each child moves towards increasingly difficult or complex responses, for example, handstand kick up – kick up to handstand with support – handstand without support – handstand from two foot take off – handstand from two foot take off with legs straight.

Complexity can be increased through requiring performance of skills in a sequence.

On apparatus, progression may be to higher pieces of apparatus or to smaller surfaces for landing or may require greater distances to be covered. The complexity of the apparatus may be increased to make greater demands of the child who is working on the construction of sequences.

3 Is the child performing with increasing control, style and finish?

In all gymnastics actions, control must be achieved before style can be improved. Once this is achieved, the aesthetic quality of gymnastics should be stressed, with constant striving for good form, poise and finesse.

4   Is the child able to perform increasingly complex sequences of movement?
Inexperienced children find difficulty in linking more than two actions together. Over a period of time the child should progress to constructing and remembering longer and more complex sequences on both floor and apparatus.

Progression from theme to theme

If work is organised thematically, themes and tasks selected should ensure that work builds on what has gone before. Tasks can be set in relation to a number of themes and it is important that lessons do not degenerate into repetition of work already covered. Questions asked above should also be asked when comparing one block of work with another.

How to improve work

Whichever method of presentation is used, the teacher may wish to:

(a)   improve the quality of the performance;
(b)   obtain greater variety and range in the work being done.

(a)   How can quality of work be improved?

1   Demand worthwhile standards. Children will not generally work to the limits of their ability unless given positive encouragement.

2   Praise and encourage whenever possible, but not for the sake of it. Praise too freely given is soon devalued in the eyes of the class. On the other hand, praise as positive reinforcement is a more effective weapon than censure.

3   Recognise and acknowledge progress, however slight.

4   Comment on the good and bad points which are emerging so that the class can recognise that you know what you want and are aware of whether it is being produced or not

'You are jumping much higher now but don't forget to control the landings.'
'You are holding the balances much better now but see if you can improve the finish of your work.'

5   Coach individuals as well as the class as a whole, to encourage them to produce the best possible performance or to point out a particular aspect of technique which will help them to succeed.

'John you could get more height in that dive roll now.'
'Mary, you will be able to hold your headstand better if you put your head and hands in triangle.'

Are your legs straight? Are your toes pointed?

6   Ask questions to stimulate thought.

'What will help you land more lightly?'
'What will help you to hold a balanced position?'
'How can you jump higher?'

7 Ask questions to stimulate greater effort.

'Are your legs straight?'
'Are your toes pointed?'
'Can you jump any higher?'

8 Give opportunity for repetition and practice. This is a feature of every learning process and is essential to progress.

9 Concentrate on one aspect of movement.

'Think about landing lightly.'
'Try to use your arms to take you high in the air.'

10 Use demonstrations to show something well done or to demonstrate a particular point which is being stressed.

'Notice how Jane keeps her legs straight.'
'Look at the position of John's head and hands.'

Demonstrations may be combined with questioning.

'Why does Mary land lightly?'
'What helps Paul to keep his balance?'

How can the teacher extend the range of movement?

1 Give opportunity for exploration and discovery *where this is needed*. This is helpful for less experienced children who are still discovering the potential of their own bodies. It is less necessary for the more experienced class.

2 Teacher stimulation to prevent pupils from continuing to practise the same movement.

'Now show me a different way.'
'How can you vary what you are doing?'
'Can you use another part of your body?'
'Can you vary the speed of your movement?'
'Can you go in a different direction?'
'Do you have to be the right way up?'
'Use a different piece of your apparatus.'

3 Comment on the work being produced. A common fault among inexperienced teachers is setting a task and leaving the class working, with no indication of whether they are producing relevant answers. Appropriate comments can indicate to a child that her work is along the right lines and may also prompt others to try the same or a similar idea.

'John is doing a headstand where his legs are apart. Perhaps some others of you could try that idea.'
'Mary's roll finishes in a straddle. How many of you can do that?'

4   Question and answer. Questions in 2 were used to stimulate movement. At a later stage, asking whether anyone can think of any other ideas may enable a child to offer a solution which no one else has shown but which she cannot perform himself.

5   Use demonstration with:
   (a)   a single pupil to show a particular idea:
         'Look at the way Jane has solved this problem.
   (b)   two pupils to show contasting ideas:
         'Watch John and Peter. They have found two ideas which answer the task which are quite different.'
   (c)   a group of pupils so that the class can observe a range of possibilities.

6   By limiting the task set, so that the class works on a range of possibilties. Limitations may be placed on:
   (a)   body parts used:
         'Now find ways of balancing so that only two points are touching the floor.'
   (b)   body shape;
   (c)   speed;
   (d)   direction of movement:
         'Now use your apparatus so that you finish facing in a different direction.'
   (e)   use of apparatus limited in some way;
   (f)   level of movement;
   (g)   type of movement:

         'Let me see every one jump to turn round.'
         'Everyone practise taking their weight on their hands.'

         These factors may be used singly or in combination:
         'Balance using only your *hands* and your *feet* so that you show a *wide* body shape.'

7   Use of these techniques should bring the class to a realisation and understanding of the factors which affect movement and which influence all movement. This should enable them to assess the possibilties within a task with relatively little guidance from the teacher. Once this stage is reached, the time spent on the exploration phase of a theme will be much less, with correspondingly more time available for development.

7 Apparatus work

Work with apparatus both large and small provides opportunity for new challenges and for the adaptation of work done on the floor to the new situation created by the introduction of apparatus. Large apparatus presents challenge and excitement to most children and the opportunity to experiment and discover the possibilities of such apparatus is valuable. It should, however, be remembered that once the initial period of exploration is over, then tasks must be set so that the work carried out in the apparatus section of the lesson is purposeful and of high quality.

Because children usually enjoy using apparatus and find it exciting, it is easy for the this part of the lesson to degenerate into activity without any teaching or progression. Few schools have sufficient apparatus to enable the teacher to give groups identical apparatus arrangements (if this is desired). Consequently, even if the same task is set for the whole class, different apparatus will produce variations in response. This makes considerable demands on the teacher if good quality movement is to be achieved and progress maintained. In setting out, using and putting away apparatus organisation is clearly essential. The selection and arrangement of the apparatus used needs careful consideration so that the challenges offered are appropriate to the work being demanded. This chapter looks at the organisation and handling of apparatus, at safety factors in the use of apparatus, and at selection and arrangement of suitable pieces of apparatus for particular kinds of work.

Organisation and handling of apparatus

It is the responsibility of the teacher to ensure that a safe gymnastics environment is provided. The following points should be observed:

1 Discipline and control are essential in all lessons.

2 Pupils must be aware of safety rules and the teacher must constantly enforce these.

3 Apparatus should only be used by pupils after it has been checked by the teacher. If a class uses a piece of apparatus which is insecure or unsafe, the teacher may be held responsible for any accident which may occur.

4 Once working time on apparatus is over, pupils should not be allowed to continue to use the apparatus.

5 The floor of the gymnasium should be smooth and non-slip. (This of course applies equally to floor work.)

6 Apparatus should be checked and repaired regularly by a suitable specialist company. Broken or insecure equipment should not be used.

7 Apparatus should be positioned to avoid collisions between pupils and walls, partitions, low ceilings and so on. There must also be sufficient space for pupils to work without colliding with each other.

8 Where potentially hazardous skills are attempted, the teacher should be prepared to stand in and catch. Pupils should not be allowed to attempt such skills without the necessary support. The teacher should not attempt to teach such skills unless he has been trained to do so.

9 Pupils should be suitably dressed for the activity.

10 The teacher should familiarise himself with the operation of the various pieces of equipment available before attempting to use such equipment in a lesson.

It should also be noted that a class whose handling of apparatus appears to be good when observed being taught by an experienced teacher, will not automatically continue such good habits. Authority needs to be established and respect gained, before a class can be safely left to handle large apparatus with a minimum of supervision.

Teachers are often told that classes have been taught to get out all or some of the large apparatus available. It is as well to bear in mind that this does not mean that they will remember or that they will have used such apparatus in the immediate past.

Constant reminder and revision is necessary, particularly with groups whose attention span is limited or whose concentration is poor.

When in doubt err on the side of safety.

A suggested procedure for getting out apparatus

(Ultimately, the way in which a class is trained to handle apparatus will depend upon the preference of the individual teacher, particularly in such matters as the extent to which he wishes to give the pupils responsibility and choice of action. The procedure suggested here would be a suitable starting point with an unknown class.)

1   Before the lesson

Arrange apparatus so that later organisation is made as straightforward as possible. It may be possible to go into the gymnasium before the start of the lesson in which case the room can be prepared in advance. If not, try to set the class working while you quickly arrange the room, i.e:

(a)   Put horses, boxes, etc. at the side of the gymnasium close to where they will eventually be needed, or at least get them out of the apparatus store and put them at the end of the gym.

(b)   Put mats ready in an accessible place. Ideally, have a pile of mats in each corner of the gym so that there is no need for queuing.

(Children can be taught to carry out both of these tasks on first entering the gym.)

2   During the lesson

Work to a routine.
Always stress safety before speed.
When getting out large apparatus follow the routine below.

(a)   Put away any mats or small apparatus which will not be needed. Move the rest close to its new position.

(b)   Adjust size of working groups if necessary and sit class down in groups where their apparatus is to go.

(c)   Tell each group exactly what they are to get out and how it is to be arranged. Do not let any group begin to get out apparatus until you have told everyone what they are to have and made sure that they have heard by questioning them. With younger children give specific tasks to each member of the group, for example, 'Jane and Mary get out the bars, Mark and Peter fetch a bench, Sarah and Paul rearrange the mats.'

The use of apparatus cards with a clearly drawn diagram can save considerable time although they will not completely remove the need for explanation.

(d)   Remind groups how to handle their particular apparatus, i.e. the order in which the bars come out, and the need to ensure that the upright is bolted into the floor before getting the bars down. Remind groups how many people are needed to get horses and boxes out and how the wheels operate, or, if there are no wheels, how to carry them, Remind groups how wall bars or window ladders come out and how to make sure that they are bolted into place before attaching any other apparatus, for example inclined forms, to them.

(e)   Tell groups to sit down beside their apparatus as soon as it is out. If a class is well-trained they can be given a task on the floor when they have got out their apparatus (space permitting) – the problem is to make sure that no one uses apparatus until you have had a chance to check it. Whichever way is chosen it is important to be strict about forbidding classes to climb onto apparatus before they have been given permission and to *make sure that this rule is enforced.*

(f)   While groups are getting out apparatus, position yourself so that you can see everyone. If you have to help with an awkward piece of apparatus, try to avoid turning your back on the rest of the class. Do *not* disappear into the apparatus store – if you stand at the entrance you can direct operations both in the store and in the main body of the gymnasium.

(g)   Check that each piece of apparatus is:
(i)   safely positioned in relation to other groups and the walls;
(ii)   correctly set up.

(h)   Set the task and start the class working.

3   At the end of the lesson

(a)   Sit the class down on the floor while you remind them of the order in which things are to be put away.

(b)   All benches, etc. must be unhooked from large apparatus first. Mats and benches will have to be moved or put away before bars or window ladders can be put away. Remind again of the way in which apparatus is to be handled, also of the number of people needed to carry various pieces of equipment. The best way of reminding the class is to ask them to tell you.

(c)   Stress safety before speed.

(d)   Set a task to be done on the floor once the apparatus is away and see that it is done.

(e)   Position yourself so that you can see everyone while the apparatus is being moved. Be ready to give a hand with awkward or stiff pieces, for example, putting boxes onto their wheels, unbolting window ladders.

When an apparatus arrangement is being used for several lessons, groups should always get out apparatus with which they are familiar. Either they get out the apparatus they put away at the end of the previous lesson and then move on to a new arrangement, or move on at the end of the lesson and put away the apparatus you want them to get out the next time.

Safety on apparatus

1 Apparatus arrangements should be selected and positioned with safety in mind. The class must have the necessary skill to be able to use a specific piece or group of apparatus. The apparatus itself must be positioned so that it may be used safely, that is, it must not be too near walls or other obstructions and it must not be too close to other groups.

   What is considered to be adequate and safe working space will, of course, depend upon the task being set. If the task is to travel along and off a longways box practising a specific vault, then the working space needed will be less and different to that necessary if the class were being asked to approach the box from every possible direction and to get off it using different pathways and angles.

2 Pupils should have had training and practice in receiving weight safely when landing from low apparatus *before* they are allowed to attempt this from high apparatus.

3 Crash mats are a useful safety aid, but they will *not* prevent injury if misused. They are *not* substitutes for effective support in vaulting or somersaulting (the latter should in any case only be taught by teachers trained to coach and support advanced movement and is rarely suitable for a class lesson). In many situations, their use makes control of a landing more difficult rather than easier, and for most apparatus work, suitable gymnastics mats provide adequate protection and discourage horseplay.

4 *Never* allow long dive forward rolls over apparatus. The margin of error is too small and spinal injury can too easily result from an incorrect landing.

5 Do not add forward rolls to landings involving flight until the pupils have learned to control the landing. There is a danger of looking down in flight which will cause forward rotation. If a vault has been over rotated, then the pupils will find it very difficult to roll forward safely.

6 Trampettes should only be used with older more experienced classes, and their use must be taught progressively (see p.48). Never use trampettes for forward flight to catch a Swedish beam.

7 When swinging or circling on bars or beams, fingers and thumbs should be in opposition and movement should *follow the thumbs not the fingers*.

8 Forward swing dismounts should *not* be allowed from Swedish beams. A diagonal approach and alternate hand grasp *must* be used where any forward or backward swing is likely.

Use of the trampette

Correctly used, the trampette has a great deal to offer.

Misused it can be a dangerous piece of apparatus because of its rebound potential and because children tend to be unaware of its potential dangers.

It is suitable *only* for older, experienced pupils.

Children *must* receive training in its use.

The teacher *must* supervise and constantly monitor its use.

Safety

1 The equipment must be in good order, and the metal frame must be protected by frame pads, preferably of the 'coverall' variety. It must also be correctly assembled.

2 Never allow the use of the trampette by children in stocking feet as socks tend to slip on the nylon bed.

3 Never allow recklessness or horseplay.

4 Make sure that the landing area has adequate protection.

Progressive activities

1 Stand on trampette and bounce gently with hands gripping partner's hands, wall bar, beam or horse pommels (whichever is used must be at a suitable height).

2 Do the same with a short approach (two or three steps is plenty).

3 Stand on trampette grasping end of long box and bounce to get knees or feet onto box.

4 Do the same with a short approach.

5 Use bench to approach trampette – this makes the hurdle step take off easier.

6 Trampette with mats. Jump from trampette to land balanced on mat. Do not add roll initially as this can encourage the pupil to look down in flight and thus rotate forwards.

7 The same with a short approach.

Children should *not* be allowed to attempt somersaults without correct support and progression. They are not appropriate for inclusion in a class lesson.

Support must be given to children attempting vaulting skills using trampettes, in order to ensure safety and to give confidence.

Selection of suitable apparatus arrangements

1   Apparatus must have sufficient space for safety and to enable the task set
to be completed.
   Make sure that members of the group can return to their starting point
without hindering the work of others. It may be necessary to specify the
route to be used.
   If two groups are working in opposite directions they will be able to wait
for turns together, rather than one group waiting where another is trying
to work.
   There will be many situations where there should be no need to form
queues for turns.
   In certain situations it may be advisable to group classes according to
height and provide apparatus of different heights to cater for the different
groups. Graded apparatus may alternatively be needed so that pupils may
work progressively.

2   Apparatus should be selected so that the theme for topic which is being
used may be explored and developed successfully on the apparatus as well
as on the floor, for example, if a class is working on *levels* then the
apparatus should be selected so that changes of level are encouraged.
Therefore arrangements where everything is at the same height would not
be suitable for this theme. Similarly, where different pathways are
desired, the arrangement must allow for a variety of approaches and this
has implications for the amount of room that will be needed around each
arrangement.

It is rarely possible and would in any case not always be desirable to have
the whole class working on identical apparatus arrangements, all attempting
the same task. Some thought, therefore, needs to be given to the combinations
of type of apparatus and task, so that logical progress may be made. Although
many schools may only have a single piece of various kinds of apparatus, most
have similar *types* of apparatus which may be used for an identical task or with
only very minor modifications to allow for slight differences in the possibilities
offered. For example, a school may only have one box, but by using horse, buck,
and other padded flat surfaces (possibly improvised, such as using a bench with
mat or mattress on the top), will be able to produce several arrangements
suitable for vaulting type or balancing activities. Some examples of how
apparatus may be planned are given below.

(a)   All groups use same apparatus or type of apparatus. All groups are set
the same task. Only possible when numbers are small or a lot of
apparatus is available. For example, six boxes/flat surfaces lengthways

with mats. Get onto, along and off, over apparatus using hands and feet only.

(b)   Each group is given different apparatus. All groups are set the same task. For example, double bars + mats; horse + mats; box + mats; wall bars + inclined form + mats; window ladders + mats. Get over, across, through or along apparatus using hands and feet only.

(c)   Two types of apparatus given. Two contrasting tasks set. For example, four groups on wallbars + inclined forms + mats; four groups on boxes/horses + mats. Use wallbars, forms and mats to make up a sequence showing different types of weight transference without flight. Get on/off or over boxes, etc. showing flight onto or off the apparatus.

(d)   Using eight groups, four types of apparatus are given. All groups are set the same task. For example, two groups on boxes + mats; two groups on double bars + mats; two groups on window ladders + mats; two groups on horses + mats. Use your apparatus to show twisting movements.

(e)   Apparatus as in (d). Each group set a different task. For example, get onto boxes and horses using hands and feet only and get off using a turning jump. Turn round the bar or window ladder either forwards or backwards and then twist to come down to the floor.

(f)   Each group given different apparatus. Each group set a different task. For example, bars, inclined form, mats; window ladder, box, form, mats; horse, form leading to it and away, mats; ropes, buck, mats; single bar, forms parallel with it, mats; wallbars, ropes, form, mats. Use bars and inclined form to make up a sequence as a group showing individual and assisted flight. Use window ladder arrangement to make up a group sequence showing twisting, turning and flight. Use horse arrangement to practise individual vaulting skills. Use ropes and buck to make up a sequence in twos showing matching actions. Use bar and forms to work out a synchronised groups sequence. Use wallbars and ropes to make up individual sequences showing flight and balance.

In the above examples an initial task only is given. Where different apparatus arrangements are used, the same task cannot be given to the whole class indefinitely, because it needs to be wide enough to cater for the differing demands made by the various pieces of apparatus. As a result, the task will eventually be too wide for purposeful work and progression to be achieved. In order to increase skill and to produce high quality work, the pupils need to work within a tightly constrained situation with an element of choice to cater for individual differences and to encourage a personal response if this is desired.

8 Teaching aids – the use of work cards

Work sheets are commonly used in classroom lessons but are utilised less frequently in practical situations. They can be a powerful and useful teaching aid, extending the amount of knowledge, information and ideas available to the pupil. Work cards are particularly valuable when working with the mixed ability groups which constitute most physical education classes, as pupils can move on to a new card when they are ready, or work through as many tasks on a card as their ability allows.

This chapter contains a selection of work cards and task cards which have been used with children of varied age and ability. Cards may simply offer a pictorial model or stimulus or may also include written instructions, questions or problems. The latter types are more limited in their use, both because the language needs to be suited to the pupils who are to use them and possibly because their instructions are more specific. They have the advantage over pictures alone of giving more information and the possibility of setting a number of challenges using the same picture or pictures as stimulus. Pupils may thus be able to work independently of the teacher for some time. Cards which are simply pictorial may be more useful to the teacher who wishes to use them as a starting point or who wishes to set a variety of tasks. The same card may be used with different ages and abilities by using different tasks with it, appropriate to the different groups.

Cards may be used for various purposes including the following:

1 To provide a model for pupils to match, for example, forward roll, different balances, a short sequence.

    Where a reciprocal teaching style is chosen, cards may be used so that children teach each other, freeing the teacher to concentrate on those in difficulty. The education potential of giving the class the opportunity to play the role of both teacher and pupil is considerable (see cards 1–10, 17–19).

2 To provide a progressive series of models by allowing pupils to move on once one card has been used satisfactorily with, for example, increasingly difficult balances, increasingly difficult sequences.

3 To provide a range of ideas, for example, different starts and finishes to rolls, different ways out of a handstand, different balances (see cards 11–16, 20, 31).

4 To promote a range of responses through setting challenges, for example, by providing a picture of a starting point and a number of tasks (see cards 32–36.)

5 To encourage progression from a given starting point by, for example, showing a simple pictorial sequence to be copied together with a number of challenges which add further dimensions or which ask the pupil to continue the sequence with actions of her choice.

Index of work cards

The work cards on pp. 102–22 may be photocopied for use in the classroom.

Card 1 Forward roll

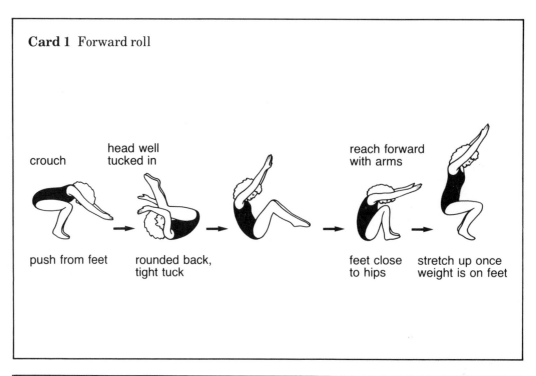

crouch   head well
tucked in   reach forward
with arms

push from feet   rounded back,
tight tuck   feet close
to hips   stretch up once
weight is on feet

Card 2 Backward roll

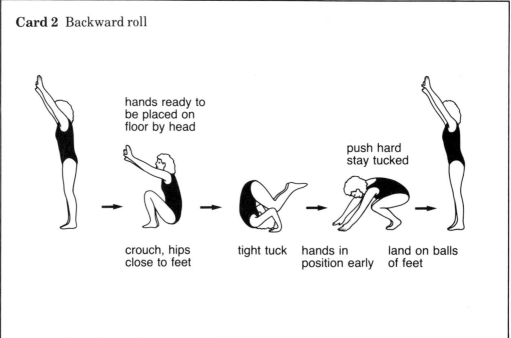

hands ready to
be placed on
floor by head

push hard
stay tucked

crouch, hips
close to feet   tight tuck   hands in
position early   land on balls
of feet

Card 3 Forward roll to straddle

Card 4 Backward roll to straddle

Card 5 Sideways roll

Card 6 Circle roll

Card 7 Headstand

walk feet up
towards hands,
on toes

head and hands
in triangle,
push on hands,
lift feet off floor

straight back,
balance before
trying to straighten
legs

Card 8 Handstand

reach forward with
hands, and place
on floor

hands shoulder width
apart, arms straight,
fingers forward
swing first leg up

look at floor
keep back straight

Card 9 Cartwheel

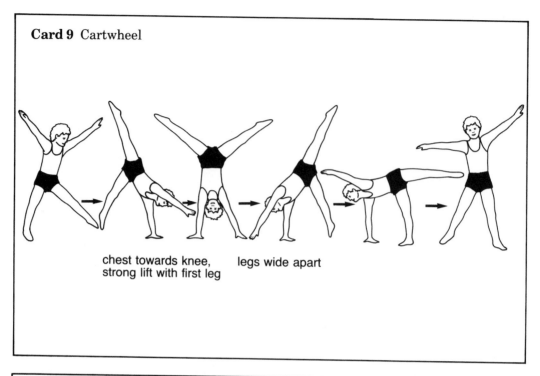

chest towards knee,
strong lift with first leg

legs wide apart

Card 10 Handstand forward roll

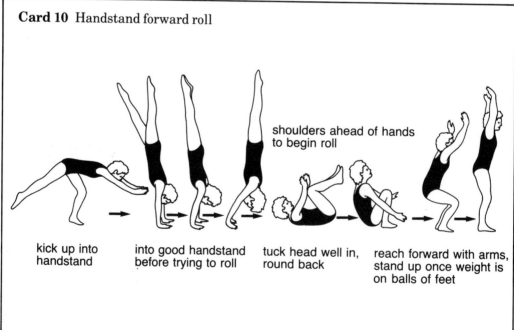

shoulders ahead of hands
to begin roll

kick up into
handstand

into good handstand
before trying to roll

tuck head well in,
round back

reach forward with arms,
stand up once weight is
on balls of feet

Card 11 Supporting weight on large surfaces

Card 12 Supporting weight on large surfaces

Card 13 Balances using hands and feet

Card 14 Balances using hands and feet

Card 15 More balances

Card 16 More balances

Card 17 Sequence 1

backward roll to straddle

lift to headstand

half turn jump

down to crouch

Card 18 Sequence 2

dive forward roll

into headstand

roll out onto one foot

cartwheel

Card 19 Sequence 3

pike down   into arabesque   forward roll

stretch jump   into second forward roll

Card 20

Into a forward roll

Into a forward roll

Card 21

Card 22

From a forward roll

Card 23

From a forward roll

Card 24

Into a backward roll

Card 25

Into a backward roll

Card 26

From a backward roll

Card 27

From a backward roll

Card 28

Beginning a handstand

Card 29

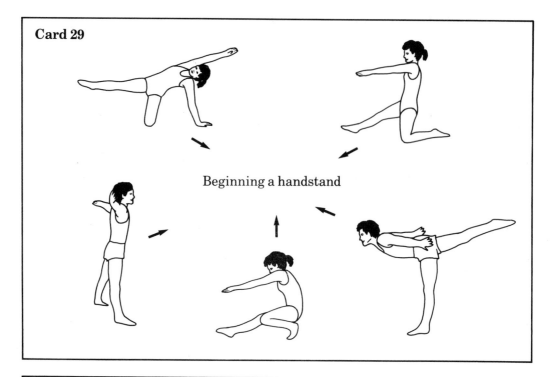

Beginning a handstand

Card 30

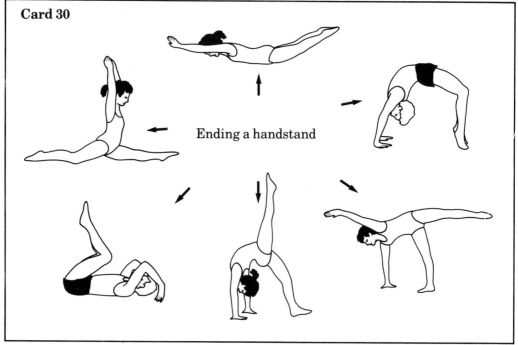

Ending a handstand

Card 31

Ending a handstand

Card 32

From this starting position can you:

1. roll sideways?
2. roll backwards?
3. roll forwards?
4. take your weight on your hands?

Card 33

From this starting position can you:

1. roll forwards?
2. roll backwards?
3. handstand or cartwheel?

Card 34

From this starting position can you:

1. roll sideways to finish in the same position?
2. roll backwards onto one foot or to straddle?
3. lie flat and return to the same position slowly?

Card 35

From this starting position can you:

1. roll backwards?
2. get onto feet and stretch jump?
3. get onto knees, crouch and headstand?
4. roll backwards onto one knee?

Card 36

From this starting position can you:

1. roll forwards?
2. come down to a straddle stand?
3. come down and roll backwards?
4. come down and stretch jump?

Card 37

Can you hold both these balances?

Now join the two balances together

1. using a roll
2. using a spinning movement
3. taking your weight on your hands

Card 38

Now hold these two balances.

Now join these two balances together

1. using a forward roll
2. using a handstand
3. using a backward roll and a jump

Card 39

Can you hold these two balances?

Now join the two balances together

1. using a roll
2. using a spinning movement
3. taking your weight on your hands

Card 40

Now hold these two balances.

Now join these two balances together

1. using a backward roll
2. using a turning jump
3. using a forward roll and a jump

Card 41

Can you hold these five balances?

Choose four of them to join together to make a sequence.
Use different actions to join the balances together.
You could use spins, rolls, steps, cartwheels, handstands, jumps.

Card 42

Can you hold these five balances?

Choose four of them to make a sequence.
Use different actions to join the balances together.
You could use spins, rolls, steps, cartwheels, handstands, jumps.

Bibliography

ANDREWS, J. (1978) *Essays on Physical Education and Sport*. Wakefield: Lepus Books.

BILBROUGH, A. and JONES, P. (1973) *Developing Patterns in Physical Education*. London: Hodder & Stoughton.

BOARD OF EDUCATION. (1909) *The Syllabus of Physical Exercises for Schools*. London: HMSO.

COPE, J. (1967) *Discovery Methods in Physical Education*. Walton-on-Thames: Nelson.

DES (1978) *Curriculum 11–16: Supplementary Papers*. London: HMSO.

GROVES, R. (1973) 'Sporting doubts about educational gymnastics'. *British Journal of Physical Education*, 14, 4.

LCC (1962) *Educational Gymnastics: A Guide for Teachers*. London: LCC.

MACE, R. and BENN, B. (1982) *Gymnastics Skills*. London: Batsford Books.

MAULDEN, E. and LAYSON, J. (1979) *Teaching Gymnastics*, 2nd edition. Plymouth: MacDonald & Evans.

MINISTRY OF EDUCATION (1952) *Moving and Growing*. London: HMSO.

MINISTRY OF EDUCATION (1953) *Planning the Programme*. London: HMSO.

MORISON, R. (1956) *Educational Gymnastics*. London: PEA.

MORISON, R. (1969) *A Movement Approach to Gymnastics*. London: Dent.

MOSSTON, M. (1981) *Teaching Physical Education*, 2nd edition. London: Merrill.

MUNROW, A.D. (1963) *Pure and Applied Gymnastics*. London: Edward Arnold.

LEARMOUTH, J. and WHITAKER, K. (1976) *Movement in Practice*. Huddersfield: Schofield & Sims.

SMITH, T. (1984) *Gymnastics – A Mechanical Understanding*. London: Hodder & Stoughton.

WILLIAMS, J. (1973) *Themes for Educational Gymnastics*. Wakefield: Lepus Books.

WRIGHT, J. (1980) Association of Principals of Women's Colleges of Physical Education, Conference paper, Nonington College.

Index